THE QUIXTAR REVOLUTION

THE QUIXTAR REVOLUTION

DISCOVER THE NEW

HIGH-TECH, HIGH-TOUCH

WORLD OF MARKETING

COY BAREFOOT

PRIMA PUBLISHING

PRIMA PUBLISHING and colophon are registered trademarks of Prima Communications, Inc.

All products mentioned are the property of their respective companies.

Library of Congress Cataloging-in-Publication Data

Barefoot, Coy.
    The Quixtar revolution : discover the new high-tech, high-touch world of marketing / Coy Barefoot.
        p. cm.
    Includes bibliographical references and index.
    ISBN 0-7615-2338-3
        1. Electronic commerce. I. Title.

    HF5548.32 .B37 2000
    658.8'00285—dc21

    00 01 02 03 04 05 HH 10 9 8 7 6 5 4
Printed in the United States of America

How to Order

Single copies may be ordered from Prima Publishing, 3000 Lava Ridge Court, Roseville, CA 95661; telephone (800) 632-8676. Quantity discounts are also available. On your letterhead, include information concerning the intended use of the books and the number of books you wish to purchase.

Visit us online at www.primalifestyles.com

For Alison,
dreams do come true

CONTENTS

PART TWO
High Touch

ACKNOWLEDGMENTS

I WISH TO express my heartfelt gratitude to a number of people who made significant contributions to this project. Foremost among these are the men and women who took time out of their busy schedules to entertain my many questions—particularly the business leaders affiliated with Quixtar: Andy Andrews, Jim Dornan, Brad Doyle, Jim Floor, Bill Florence, Tim Foley, Hal Gooch, Bert Gulick, Fred Harteis, Brian Hays, Paul Miller, Bo Short, Jody Victor, Chuck Vogt, and Dexter Yager.

I am indebted to John Parker as well, for his tireless help and assistance. And thanks to Congressman Boucher, for sharing his thoughts about the development of the Internet and ecommerce. I am also grateful to Kim Davis, Connie Altschwager, Lisa Shannon, Robin Luymes, and John Gartland for their timely and critical support.

Many thanks to the incredibly talented team at Prima: Ben Dominitz, Susan Silva, Colby Olds, Andrew Vallas, and Patricia Waldygo.

I especially appreciate Bo and Sandy Short for opening the doors and for giving this project wings. And I want to recognize Matt Sweetanos for his unselfish help; this book would not have gotten very far without him.

I also want to give thanks to close friends and family for their constant encouragement and support.

Finally I would like to thank my wife, Alison, who skillfully edited early drafts of this manuscript and offered invaluable insight every step along the way.

THE YEAR WAS 1969. Despite a booming economy and low unemployment, America was torn over the war in Vietnam. Richard Nixon was enjoying his first year in the White House. Hundreds of thousands of people converged on a dairy farm in upstate New York for the Woodstock Music and Art Fair. Hit movies of the year included *Butch Cassidy and the Sundance Kid, Midnight Cowboy,* and *Easy Rider.*

It was the year that television unveiled *Sesame Street, Mr. Roger's Neighborhood, The Brady Bunch,* and *Marcus Welby M.D.* The New York Jets won Super Bowl III, and the New York Mets celebrated their first World Series victory. The radio was playing "Hot Fun in the Summertime," "Raindrops Keep Falling on My Head," and Merle Haggard's "Okie from Muskogee."

This was also the Year of the Moon, when Neil Armstrong and Buzz Aldrin climbed down from the *Apollo 11* lunar module and stepped onto the surface of the moon for the first time. As people watched and listened to broadcasts of the historic event around the world, there was a sense that it was both the fulfillment of an old dream as well as the beginning of a new era

On Monday, September 1, 1969, another historic event took place that would prove to have as profound an impact on the world as the moon walk. On that day a uniquely designed computer was flown from Massachusetts to California, where it was delivered to a research facility at UCLA. A forklift trundled the massive computer into the building and set it gently into place as a small crowd of eager students and engineers looked on.

That computer—known as an Interface Message Processor, the first of its kind—was the beginning of what would one day be known as the Internet. Exactly one month later, on October 1, 1969, the computer "talked" to another computer at the Stanford Research Institute. It was a rough start, with computers crashing and gadgets constantly having to be tweaked and reworked. But the experiment was a success. It was the first time in history that people at remote locations had communicated through computers. The world would never be the same again.

FAST FORWARD THIRTY years. The Internet heralds a new era in human history. The World Wide Web and electronic commerce have rapidly become forces of great change in our society, bringing with them a host of new challenges and new opportunities.

Exactly thirty years to the day after the Internet began to come alive, history was made once again. Quixtar.com opened its doors at 4:37 P.M. on Wednesday, September 1, 1999. The Quixtar revolution—a quantum leap forward in marketing and business—had begun. The Internet and ecommerce would never be the same again.

What is Quixtar? There are many ways to answer that question. Quixtar.com has been described as a Personal Shopping Portal, as the world's largest online shopping mall, as Tridigital Commerce, as a new business model created specifically for the Internet, and as the premiere business opportunity of the new millennium. It's been called the pioneering model of high-tech/high-touch marketing, as well as the paradigm for business in the 21st century. Quixtar is a new archetype for a new period in history. It is all of these and more.

THE WORLD HAS been waiting for Quixtar. Between midnight and noon on September 1, the Quixtar.com Web site received over 20 million hits—approximately the population of the New York metropolitan area. Millions of people, incorrectly believing that the site would launch at precisely 12 midnight, starting knocking on the virtual door to get in—and they didn't stop.

Late that afternoon, Quixtar flung open its doors to the world. As this book is being written the site is registering 30 to 40 million hits a day, and is one of the most successful ecommerce sites on the World Wide Web. Shortly after the historic launch of Quixtar.com, I spoke with Ken McDonald, the Senior Vice President and Managing Director of Quixtar.

"This is a momentous event, and a first for the Internet," Ken said proudly. "Never before has a Web site been launched with this much traffic from day one. Quixtar.com is the start of something totally new in ecommerce. We're making history, and it's an incredible honor to be a part of this.

"We had some technical challenges the first few days, which was unexpected but nothing we couldn't handle. We got the best people right on it, and have been constantly fine-tuning the infrastructure to prevent any bottlenecks. We have one of the best Web teams in the country focused on nothing but improving the speed and performance of the site on a daily basis. If any other challenges should come up, we're ready for them."

For nearly a year, Ken and his team at Quixtar—which included an Internet development group of over a hundred talented designers—had been working to meet the September 1 launch date.

"Yes, there are some of us here who could use some sleep," he said with a laugh. "We've been pulling some late nights over the past few weeks to make sure everything is running smoothly. But when you look at the site, and see how well it's all put together, you know it's been worth it. We've been real fortunate with the team we put together. Everyone came through and has done a terrific job."

With the site now up and running, the Quixtar team is focused on new heights. As Ken explained: "Now the work really starts. We've got all new goals laid out and upgrades planned for the site. We're bringing on new partner stores as we speak, and broadening the product lines. Quixtar is only going to get bigger, faster, more accessible, and more user-friendly as time goes on."

IN THIS BOOK we're going to explore the new world of high-tech, high-touch marketing as pioneered by Quixtar.com. We'll focus on two specific questions: What is Quixtar? And why is it so revolutionary? We will look closely at both the high-tech and high-touch sides of Quixtar.

In Chapter 1 we're going to consider the Internet Revolution of which Quixtar is a part. The Net is just the latest in a series of great periods of innovation and change in human history. We'll take a look at some of these historical shifts to see what lessons we can learn about the Internet and Quixtar.

Chapter 2 presents the history of computers in ten easy steps. And in Chapter 3 we will explore the history of the Internet and take a close-up look at the booming world of ecommerce.

In Chapter 4 we'll consider the historic roots of Quixtar.com. Then in Chapter 5 we will take a behind-the-scenes look at what went in to the making of Quixtar. A handy list of frequently asked questions about Quixtar.com rounds out this chapter.

Next, in Chapter 6, we will reflect on all the advantages that make Quixtar truly unique and successful. And Chapter 7 focuses on why Quixtar.com is the new model of business for the 21st century.

WHILE WRITING THIS book I was very fortunate to have had a series of one-on-one conversations with some of the top, global business leaders affiliated with Quixtar.com. Each of these business owners, all of them enormously successful entrepreneurs, spoke candidly about the unique experience and ground-breaking opportunity that is Quixtar. I was so impressed and enlightened by their remarks that rather than edit their comments to brief snippets or soundbytes, I decided to let you "listen in" on the greater part of each conversation. Collected here for the first time are the thoughts and insights of some of the most progressive, visionary leaders of the Quixtar business. These conversations will appear throughout the book.

OUR JOURNEY THROUGH the world of Quixtar will be quite an adventure. Along the way, we will talk to a 107-year-old woman, visit the Wizard of Oz, take a ride through the solar system, and find out what the history of bicycles can tell us about the future. We're going to have a lot of fun.

PART ONE

HIGH TECH

CHAPTER ONE

You Are Here:
The Internet and
10,000 Years of Innovation

WHAT?" THE MAN asked me, his head tilting slightly. "Ecommerce," I answered. "*Electronic* commerce, digital commerce—you know, computers, the Internet, all of that."

"Hmm . . ." he said slowly. Then he shook his head and chortled: "I'm sure it's interesting to you. I know a lot of people are talking about that stuff. But if you ask me, that's exactly what's wrong with the world today: *computers.*"

"They're what's *wrong* with the world?" I repeated with a laugh.

"Yeah, computers are speeding things up too fast. By the time you think you understand something, it all changes. Who can keep up? Everything is changing too fast. Who can live like that?"

I nodded quietly. The man, a forty-something friend of mine who runs a small mechanic shop, looked out the window across a broad parking lot. He turned his face into the sunshine and squinted.

JUST A FEW days later I had a similar chat with a woman in a grocery store. A friend of a friend, she had heard I was working on a new book and asked me what it was about.

"Ecommerce," I told her. "It's about an Internet company called Quixtar that's going to revolutionize business."

Her expression crumpled. "I don't know much about computers," she said apologetically. "They scare me."

"What scares you about them?"

"They're just intimidating. They confuse me. And they're too expensive. Besides, that whole Internet thing, I just don't know what to make of it."

I nodded again.

THESE TWO CONVERSATIONS, both of which took place in the same week not too long ago, were real learning experiences for me. There I was—all fired up about ecommerce, the Internet, and especially Quixtar.com—absolutely convinced that we stand at the threshold of an exciting new era in human history and that Quixtar is leading the way.

But here were two people, both of them intelligent and hard-working, who didn't really understand the first thing about what was happening to the world around them. The question "E what?" summed it up very nicely. They were aware that *something* was going on—all you have to do is watch the nightly news or pick up a newspaper to appreciate that. No matter where you turn, someone is talking about the wonders of computers and the fast-changing world of the Internet.

But as for really understanding what all this means to each of us personally, to our families, to our communities, and to our society as a whole, they didn't get it. They were unaware that the innovation of the Internet represents a pivotal moment in history no less momentous than the Industrial Revolution. This is the great transformation of our time. Like it or not, the world *is* changing—and you're going to be a part of it.

The age in which we now live is a promising time in human history, full of unprecedented opportunities to improve our lives. How we react, and what we do with the possibilities we encounter, will be up to each of us. Those who pay attention to cultural trends and emerging technologies, who are aware of the lessons of history, and who are willing to step forward and seize the opportunity that these new innovations offer will enjoy the rewards that their hard work brings. Those who don't take steps now to conquer their fear of new technologies will miss out on one of the greatest eras of opportunity in human history.

> They were unaware that the innovation of the Internet represents a pivotal moment in history no less momentous than the Industrial Revolution.

LET'S FACE IT: All the reports about new technology can be, for many people, quite confusing and a little scary. Most of us are too busy or too stressed out these days to have the time and energy to think about what's going on. For some people, the Internet is just another item on a list of things they don't have time for.

More and more people feel alienated—from their work, from each other, and from the times in which we live. Frustration, anger, confusion, intimidation, fear—these are all common reactions in an age when the application of emerging technologies brings massive change to our society. So if you feel a little perplexed about this Internet or Information Revolution, just know that you are not alone.

Momma's Washtub

IT'S JUST AFTER four on a late summer afternoon, and Mrs. Rebecca McGinness is sitting quietly at her kitchen table, sifting through a stack of cards and letters from family and friends. The door to the back porch stands open, and the songs of blue jays and cardinals drift through the screen.

A dear friend of mine, Mrs. McGinness understands history better than anyone I know. You see, she was born in 1892. As this book is being written, Mrs. McGinness is preparing to celebrate her 107th birthday. She lives just a few miles from my house, and I often stop by to say hello and chat. She holds court in her kitchen, where she usually sits in a red-cushioned chair at the end of a long table.

Mrs. McGinness was born in Charlottesville, Virginia, in 1892, just three days before Grover Cleveland was elected president. She remembers well the stories her father and grandmother (both of whom had been slaves) told her about life as it used to be. Mrs. McGinness has also personally witnessed the drama of the twentieth century—from horses and buggies to space travel; from the Victrola to the Sony compact disc; from ink wells to Microsoft Word.

"In the house where I was born," she says slowly, leaning forward in her chair, "we had kerosene lamps, no electricity. We didn't have any running water or plumbing either, just a hydrant in the backyard. We didn't even have a sink in the kitchen, just a big tin wash basin. We cooked and kept the house warm with wood and coal. That was it."

Mrs. McGinness tells me it's normal for people to be frightened of change. When I say that some folks are nervous about how computers are changing the world, she smiles and shakes her head.

"That's nothing new," she says. "Let me tell you about my momma. I can remember my father came home one day with a brand new washtub—even had a crank on the side so you could wring the clothes out. But my momma didn't want it. She wanted to keep on using her *washboard* just like she was used to. But one day she gave that new washtub a try, and she really liked it. She was tickled to death over it, once she realized how easy it was. She didn't want electricity either, said lightning would strike the house if we put those wires in there. She didn't want gas, said it would kill us. She wanted to stay with the coal and wood she was used to. But when I graduated from the Hampton Institute in 1915, I was a modern girl. And I came home to Charlottesville and had all those modern things put into my momma's house. She didn't want them. But you know, she was so tickled once she got used to them."

Mrs. McGinness pauses, sits back in her chair, and sips on a glass of water. She dabs her lips with a tissue and clears her throat.

"Those computers are just like my momma's new washtub," she sighs. "There's always something new coming along. Times always change. And you have to keep learning new things all the time. That's the way God wants it—wants us to keep learning and keep trying and keep understanding new things. You know, this is such a wonderful world. It really is a wonderful world. But you've got to change with it and grow with it, or it will leave you behind."

A Whirlwind Tour of the History of Innovation

THE FIRST STEP we will take together toward understanding and appreciating this exciting age in which we live—and the truly path-breaking role of Quixtar—is to put the Internet into historical context. In this first chapter we'll get some perspective on the technological revolution we are witnessing at the dawn of the twenty-first century.

If there is one message I want you to get from this chapter, it is this: The period of technological innovation and cultural transformation we now live in—dramatic and momentous though it may be—is actually just the latest in a long line of similar developments that have shaped and molded societies throughout human history. Every once in a while, new technologies emerge and are applied in such a way that all aspects of society are affected, posing new challenges and offering immense opportunities for those who are paying attention. Right now, at this moment—this is one of those times. Pay attention.

The Beginning of Society

All throughout human history, new ideas, innovations, and the novel uses of emerging technologies have transformed and reshaped the societies in which our ancestors have lived. Let's consider a few key examples.

Things really got rolling between 12,000 and 10,000 years ago (approximately 10,000 to 8,000 B.C.), when bands of hunter-gatherers began herding and breeding animals and cultivating crops for the first time. For many thousands of years, human beings had hunted wild animals and gathered naturally growing fruits and cereals. In regions abundant with wild grains—especially the area in Southwest Asia known as the Fertile Crescent (parts of Iran, Iraq, Turkey, and Syria)— new tools had been developed to help collect and process wild plants. Flint-bladed sickles, woven baskets, stone mortars and pestles, and clay storage pots were all created to make the gathering of grains and fruits easier. Farming and food production evolved over time and was made possible thanks to the use of these tools.

The domestication of animals—notably, dogs, sheep, goats, pigs, and cows—began about this time as well, initiating a practice that has continued into the twentieth century. (Hamsters, for example, were not domesticated as pets until the 1930s.) Like farming, techniques for breeding captive animals were improved over time. People gradually became more dependent on the materials and foodstuffs these new ways provided. The complete reliance on hunting and gathering as a lifestyle progressively became less and less common. In our lifetime, as the last of the great traditional societies adapt new methods and technologies, we are now witnessing the end of hunting and gathering as a way of life in the world.

THE DOMESTICATION OF plants and animals 10,000 years ago set into motion the first great transformation in human society. Farming and breeding livestock ushered in a totally new era in human civilization—a process that anthropologists refer to as the "rise of social complexity." This is a very appropriate phrase, because that's exactly what happened—social life got very complex from that point on. For tens of thousands of years, human societies had been small, predominantly nomadic bands made up of about thirty to fifty people. A closely knit kinship system united the band, which depended on reciprocity and the ritualized exchange of goods. By and large, there were no classes and no rulers—no chiefs and no presidents. But the sedentary, settled lifestyle that came with farming and the domestication of animals brought all of that to an end.

The most notable change that resulted was the steady growth in population, which coincided with our ancestors' adaptation to farming and keeping livestock. Over the next few thousand years, dense collections of people started living together, forming towns and villages. In some cases—such as the community of Catal Huyuk in modern Turkey, which may have had as many as 6,000 residents—the new settlements were small cities of clay- and mud-plastered homes. Societies became centralized, with chiefs, leaders, and a ruling class that assumed authority over others. Economic inequalities began to emerge—some people had more, some had less.

Other innovations of this unique era in human history (5000 to 3000 B.C.) included craft specialization. Select individuals became experts at woodworking, for example, or manufacturing pottery, or smelting copper into molds. A need for improved transportation of harvested crops and goods led to the invention of the wheel (originally constructed from three pieces of wood); and writing was developed to keep records and accounts of commerce. New trade routes flourished, increasing communication and helping to spread technologies and innovations throughout Europe and Asia.

Copper, Bronze, Iron, and Beyond

Craftsmen gradually learned that copper mixed with tin in just the right amounts rendered bronze—the production of which kicked off a new age of material production (referred to as the Bronze Age). In time, continued experiments led to the mining and smelting of iron, which was preferable to bronze since tin was often hard to come by. Artists and metallurgists refined tools that made better boats and vehicles possible—which in turn led to improved communication and ever more trade.

By 2000 B.C. the toil of thousands of slaves had created the Great Pyramids of Egypt on the sandy plains at Giza; Stonehenge was constructed about 1500 B.C.; the classic Greek temples were built by 500 B.C.; and by the time Christ was born in Jerusalem, a mighty new Roman empire had set the stage for the emergence of modern city-states.

Chinese Innovation

The next great era of innovation—following the fall of Rome around A.D. 500, the subsequent "dark ages," and the rise of the Islamic Empire—occurred in China and western Asia before and after the year A.D. 1000.

During this period, Chinese craftsmen used large blast furnaces to perfect the art of casting iron. Their remarkable innovations, at a time when most of Europe had plunged into poverty and stagnation, stand out as the hallmark of a great age of ingenuity. Chinese metallurgists turned out impressive suits of armor, iron arrowheads for crossbows, reliable and sturdy farming tools, and new construction materials such as iron roof tiles. Chinese Buddhists led in the building of giant statues and new iron bridges. There were also notable advances in irrigation, printing, gunpowder, silk and textile production, navigation, and hydraulic engineering.

Ironically, when the nomadic Mongolians—under the leadership of Ghengis Khan—invaded and conquered China in the early 1200s, they were largely successful thanks to Chinese innovations in horse harnesses, particularly the iron stirrup. The new and improved foothold left the rider with both hands free, a decisive fighting advantage when using a bow and arrow from horseback.

The Library at Toledo

In the eleventh century various Christian kingdoms in Europe, which had been isolated and divided by feudal wars during the "dark ages," reunited and began attacking Muslims to the south—beginning with well-developed Islamic cities in Spain. In A.D. 1085 the city of Toledo, Spain—the Arab center of science and philosophy—fell to the European armies of the north. This event proved to be a critical turning point in the history of the West.

Christians took control of the scholarly town and began to explore the massive Arab library that was located there. As they translated the fascinating texts into Latin, Europeans were introduced to new and foreign concepts, and impressive technologies that would revolutionize the Western world—not the least of which were the philosophy, logic, mathematics, and science of the classical Greeks.

Those who pay attention to cultural trends and emerging technologies, who are aware of the lessons of history, and who are willing to step forward and seize the opportunity that these new innovations offer will enjoy the rewards that their hard work brings. Those who don't take steps now to conquer their fear of new technologies will miss out on one of the greatest eras of opportunity in human history.

An Indian number system (which introduced the zero to Europe) was adapted and referred to as "Arabic numerals." The collected wisdom of the Arab empire—comprised of Muslim, Greek, Hindu, Chinese, and Egyptian writings—slowly spread throughout Christendom, planting the seeds for both the Renaissance and the Reformation.

Pre-Industrial Revolution
About the same time that Medieval Christians were discovering the Arab library at Toledo and waging bloody war campaigns through their Crusades against Jews and Muslim Turks, northern Europe was emerging from the "dark ages" and entering its first great age of mechanical innovation— which some scholars have described as the Western world's pre-Industrial Revolution.

Improving on the use of waterwheels and windmills in the 1100s and 1200s, Europeans learned to harness natural power as never before. The wheels, originally used to turn millstones to grind corn and grains, were adapted over time to perform a variety of functions. The great turning wheels were hooked up to camshafts (another innovation) and used to drive hammers that crushed rocks, forged iron, and beat fibers into pulp to make paper. They worked bellows to fan the flames needed for smelting iron; they cranked saws that cut wood; and they revolutionized mining by moving buckets of rock and ore. During the next few centuries, wind- and water-powered mills proliferated throughout Europe and were hooked up to run just about every mechanical procedure anyone could think of. A burst of new commerce and trade spread across the continent.

The principle invention of this pre-Industrial Age in Europe, as historian Fernand Braudel has pointed out, was that "a single engine, a single wheel—whether wind- or watermill—could transmit its momentum to several implements; not to one millstone but to two or three; not to one saw but to a saw plus a tilt-hammer; not to one pile but to a whole series." By linking wheels, cranks, pulleys, camshafts, and tools together, people multiplied the abilities of one wheel to run an entire system of machines. The power of the mechanical network was born.

Towns and villages began to grow up around the mills, just as densely populated settlements had first appeared around farming sites thousands of years earlier. The mills also helped to process the boom in agriculture that resulted when the padded horse-collar was invented in the twelfth century. Horses, previously used mainly in war, now became effective farm animals because the new device made it possible for them to pull plows and carts more easily. As during previous periods of innovation and change, opportunities brought improved commerce, trade, and new-found wealth.

Remember, the purpose of this brief history tour is to help us appreciate that every now and then in human history, there have been periods of great transformation brought on by the birth of new concepts and new technologies. The age of the Renaissance is one of the most obvious examples of a time when innovative ideas and emerging technologies drastically transformed human society.

The Renaissance

IN THE MID-1300S, Europe and Asia were tragically hit with the bubonic plague, or the "Black Death," as it was known in England, because of the dark spots that appeared on the skin of people who got sick. Transmitted by fleas from rats, the plague spread rapidly and killed 25 million people in less than five years—a third of the population of Europe. By the end of the century nearly half the European workforce had died, which sent shockwaves through society and upset the previous social order of the Medieval world.

In the 1390s, as people slowly rebounded from the horrifying effects of the epidemic, Italian merchants stepped up their investments in banking, trade, and exploration. The Medici family of Florence created an expansive network of banks throughout Europe (with a branch as far away as London), the first successful business model of its kind. At the heart of their commercial triumph was an innovative accounting system that made it possible to track expenditures, transfer credit, process checks, and balance their books, far outstripping the abilities of any other lenders. The incredible wealth and power the Medicis acquired in this new era of opportunity rocketed them to a social status previously held only by feudal lords and aristocrats. The Medicis paid close attention to the new opportunities that major changes brought their way, and they were not afraid to take advantage of them.

The Renaissance period—traditionally, the dates 1400 to 1600—began as a "rebirth" of the classical ideals of Greece and Rome but quickly evolved into a flowering of more modern achievements and progress. Art, literature, architecture, politics, philosophy—every aspect of society was somehow shaped by the advances and exhilarating promise of the Renaissance. Capitalism and individualism flourished; and an array of trading opportunities made it the "age of the entrepreneur." As new-found wealth spread to common men and women across Europe, an influential middle class developed, hungry for status and political power. The strength of the state, supported by the wealthy new middle class, began to challenge the long-established power of the Roman Catholic Church.

New values characterized this changing world: Civic life, a sense of community, and good character were paramount; commerce and social mobility took center stage. As historian James Burke has written, the Renaissance model of humankind was "independent, intelligent, adventurous, capable."

The Printing Press

The invention of the printing press stands out as perhaps the most important development during the Renaissance. The earliest printed document actually dates to about 1700 B.C. in Minoan Crete in the Mediterranean. Known as the Phaistos Disk, it is a round, baked-clay disk with lettering that has never been deciphered. Methods for printing on paper were later created in China, where Buddhist monks produced the first books using inked wooden blocks or ceramic letters imprinted on paper. But the technique was slow and tedious and certainly not meant for mass production. Koreans actually invented moveable metal type in the early 1300s, a limited experiment that failed to catch on.

In Europe during the Middle Ages, books were still created the old-fashioned way: by copying them word-by-word, image-by-image. Monks spent exhausting hours in the monasteries copying texts by hand, writing on pressed animal skins with quill pens made of bird feathers dipped in ink. Sometimes it took a year to copy one book. Monks read aloud as they copied, a hold-over from a very long oral tradition. In fact, reading silently to yourself was almost unheard of at the time and was considered a rare display of talent.

In the exciting years of the Renaissance, European craftsmen began experimenting with metal typecasting and printing.
In Germany in the year 1456, after five years of work, Johann
Gutenberg and his partner, Johann Fust, released a printed
Latin version of the Bible. In a few short years every major city
in Europe had its own printing press. Less than sixty years after
the Gutenberg Bible was published, there were over eight million printed books in circulation, and they just kept coming.
The world would never be the same again.

The Reformation

The freedom of thought and individualism that grew out of
the Renaissance, coupled with the incredible might of the printing press, led directly to a massive reform movement in the
Christian faith. On a trip to Rome in the early 1500s, a thirty-
four-year-old German monk named Martin Luther was
concerned about the corruption that he believed had contami-
nated some Church leaders. In 1517 he wrote his now famous
ninety-five theses—declarations about his views on faith and
the proper role of the Church and priests. Hoping to discuss
these ideas with his fellow monks at one of their scholarly get-
togethers, Luther nailed the ninety-five theses to the door of
the chapel, which the friars used like a bulletin board.

But what happened next altered the course of world civilization. Luther's controversial theses were picked up, printed
on the new presses, and rapidly passed around Germany.
Within a few weeks, thousands of copies were circulating
throughout Europe. Unwittingly, Luther soon found himself
at the head of a great rebellion. His revolutionary ideas—
that salvation should come through faith and not through
the judgments of Church leaders—quickly found a large

following. Armed with the passionate and intellectual ammunition that Luther's writings inspired, German princes later "protested" against the rule of Rome and argued for the freedom of religion. The Protestant movement was born.

Five Lessons from History

THE NEW TECHNOLOGIES, innovations, and ideas that burst forward in each of these periods of history had dramatic repercussions in society, bringing both challenges and opportunities. When it comes to understanding our own innovative Age of the Internet, what are the lessons that these stories from history offer us? Here are five:

1. **Change Happens**—Mrs. McGinness was right: Nothing stays the same. Change is the normal state of things, and it always has been. Whenever someone complains about computers changing the world, that is like a Stone-Age farmer grumbling about the invention of the wheel. Can't you picture it? "Back in my day we got along fine without those new-fangled wheels. All they do is speed things up too fast. Look how fast that cart is moving! Who needs to move a cart that fast? I prefer the old method of carrying the stuff on my back!" Or imagine someone in Europe in the 1200s: "Back in my day we got along fine without those new-fangled windmills. All they do is speed things up too fast. Look how fast that millstone is moving! Who needs to grind grain that fast? I prefer the old method of smashing the wheat by hand in a mortar and pestle!"

The first lesson we can draw from history is that *change does happen*—sometimes it's fast; sometimes it's slow. But it's absolutely guaranteed to take place. We now live in a period of immense change. The Internet's many applications to our daily lives represent a profound turning point in human society. Don't be caught off-guard, and don't be afraid of it. As Mrs. McGinness would say, this is a beautiful world. But it grows and changes, and you have to grow and change with it.

2. **You Matter. Yes, You!**—The common thread running through all of these magnificent ages of innovation are attentive men and women who were willing to open their minds to new possibilities and new ways of doing things. Our very success as a species on this earth, and as children of our Creator, relies on our individual willingness to adapt, to innovate, to explore, to try, and to reach beyond that which we believe to be our limits. This is certainly one of history's greatest teachings.

The course of civilization has been altered again and again by those *individuals* who paid close attention to what went on in the world around them—whether they were Chinese craftsmen experimenting with iron, medieval farmers watching waterwheels turn, or Renaissance printers who fine-tuned a new way of communicating. They were not necessarily extraordinary people with incredible talents. They carefully observed the world around them. They were willing to learn, and they were not afraid of new technologies. As we enter the twenty-first century, there is perhaps no greater lesson we can keep in mind. History emphatically teaches us that *individual men and women do matter.* Yes, one person *can* change the world.

3. **Technology Gets Around**—The wheel was invented in the Middle East over 5,000 years ago. Now every human society on the globe has benefited from its use. A thousand years ago, only the Chinese had truly mastered the art of smelting iron in blast furnaces. But those techniques are now known worldwide. At one point during the Renaissance, only a handful of people actually had printing presses. That technology is now a part of every modern society. The fundamental lesson is this: Technology gets around. It does not stand still. It wants to be where people are.

It may be hard to imagine, but not too long ago there was only one computer. Now they are everywhere. When researchers started hooking mainframes together around 1970, there were only four or five computers on that network. Now there are many millions plugged into the Internet, and the number grows exponentially each day. If the lessons of history tell us anything, it is that Internet technology will one day encompass all of human civilization. And Quixtar, which today only covers North America, will reach the entire world.

4. **The Secret Is in the Network**—Remember the waterwheels from Europe's pre-Industrial Age around

A.D.1200? It wasn't just the technology of waterwheels and windmills that made this exciting age possible. Waterwheels had already been around for hundreds of years. What was so inventive is that the moving wheels were hooked up to—or *networked* with—other machines, like hammers and saws. Likewise, in the 1400s, it wasn't the existence of one Medici-owned bank using a new accounting system that revolutionized commerce and funded the artists of the Renaissance. The key fact was that a *network* of those Medici banks had spread throughout Europe, with all the banks in communication with each other.

We saw the same process make the Reformation possible. Think about it—the mere existence of a printing press didn't circulate the teachings of Martin Luther across Europe. But a *network* of craftsmen using a multitude of printing presses, one in each major city, connected by merchants traveling regular trade routes, made that massive spiritual and cultural revolution possible. No invention exists in a vacuum. It is part of a matrix of other devices and part of a human social network.

Now, what does this say about our own day and age? Yes, a computer is an amazing invention. But a single computer is not in itself enough to transform society and usher in a new era. That was only made possible when computers were *networked* together, beginning in the 1970s, creating the Internet.

5. **Commerce Is the Key**—If history tells us one thing, it is that we should never underestimate the role that

commerce plays in shaping society. The need to move goods to market led to the creation of the wheel. The need to keep track of trade sparked the invention of writing. The powerful waterwheels and windmills in the 1200s led to a new era in business, which helped draw Europe out of the "dark ages." And improved trade routes, banking, and commercial ventures made many of the wonders of the Renaissance possible.

Emerging technologies, commercial ventures, and business opportunities have always been closely linked throughout human history. That's one reason why Internet-based electronic commerce is so significant today. Networking computers on the Internet may be the secret to innovation. But ecommerce will be the key that unlocks the true promise this technology offers our world.

You Say You Want a Revolution?

AT THIS POINT I hope that you have a better understanding of the Internet's place in history. The past has a great deal to teach us about what's going on in the present and what may be in store for us in the future, as long as we are willing to learn. History has a few more lessons up its sleeve for us.

The ecommerce age that is just beginning—this dawning era of the Internet—represents the third Great Shift in Commerce in American history. First came the Industrial Revolution of the late 1700s, and then the Corporate Revolution of the late 1800s. Both of these periods witnessed dramatic developments in technology and commerce that transformed society and created the modern world. It is absolutely critical that we take a close look at each of these revolutions to appreciate just how much the Internet will reshape society in the next few decades.

The Industrial Revolution

Some people now say that the Age of the Internet will be the New Industrial Revolution of our times. Just what was the Industrial Revolution? Well, in one sentence: the Industrial Revolution was that period in the late 1700s and early 1800s when the use of emerging technologies and new business models totally *revolutionized* industry, commerce, and society. The Industrial Revolution was that point in time when the Medieval World gave way to the Modern World. Western society was turned upside down and forever changed by new inventions and new ways of doing business. Nearly every aspect of life in society has been somehow affected by this age of innovation.

Change is the normal state of things, and it always has been. Whenever someone complains about computers changing the world, that is like a Stone-Age farmer grumbling about the invention of the wheel. Can't you picture it? "Back in my day we got along fine without those new-fangled wheels. All they do is speed things up too fast. Look how fast that cart is moving! Who needs to move a cart that fast? I prefer the old method of carrying the stuff on my back!"

FOR THE SAKE of convenience, let's say the Industrial Revolution got started in 1765, the year James Watt patented an improved steam engine. Just twenty-nine years old at the time, Watt was a Scotsman whose job it was to build scientific equipment for the University of Glasgow. The steam engine had actually been around for awhile, being used primarily to pump water from iron mines. But it had never really been all that powerful. Because Watt was experienced at repairing distilleries, he figured out a way to make the engine much more efficient. His steam engine, which left all the older models in the dust, was an instant hit.

In 1781 Watt, largely with the help of his assistant William Murdock, improved on the engine by hooking it up to a cogwheel and pulley system. The result of this new machine network was truly revolutionary. For hundreds of years—since Europe's pre-Industrial Age, which we discussed earlier— people had largely depended on waterwheels to power the simple machines on their farms and in their mills. Industry had not changed all that much during that time. But Watt's invention was a magnificent breakthrough. With the addition of a rotary network of gears and pulleys, the steam engine could run any number of machines faster, more powerfully, and more reliably than the waterwheels ever could.

BESIDES WATT'S STEAM engine, a number of other inventions made the Industrial Revolution possible. In 1792 twenty-six-year-old Eli Whitney, a recent Yale graduate, invented a cotton engine ("cotton gin" for short) that made it much easier to get seeds out of the cotton bolls. The production of cotton in the South skyrocketed from 140,000 pounds in 1791 to over 35 million pounds just ten years later.

In 1782 Englishman Henry Cort developed a way to increase iron production. For the first time, iron could be mass produced in a mold, making it cheaper to manufacture machine parts out of iron rather than wood. Cast iron, as opposed to labor-intensive wrought iron, became much more common. Mass production also boosted an unprecedented output of a variety of everyday objects—brooms, shovels, hoes, clothing, buttons, ribbons, plates, glassware, furniture, shoes, and hats. The production of goods became standardized and mechanized, relying on machines as much, if not more, than people. No longer was it necessary for the items to be handmade by craftsmen in their cottages, as they had been for generations. The craftsmen left their homes to labor in common workshops as employees.

THE INDUSTRIAL REVOLUTION also brought massive technological changes to the textile industry. Beginning in the 1760s, inventors made drastic improvements to spinning machines and looms. In 1769 Richard Arkwright, a thirty-seven-year-old English wig-maker, invented a new machine to produce cotton thread. But even more important than his invention was Arkwright's ingenious way of *organizing* workers around the machines.

At that time, British trade agents (called "factors") working overseas on plantations in India and the Caribbean were known for the incredible authority they exerted over laborers. Arkwright developed a business model based on the factors' work style—controlling employees—and combined that with the new spinning machines in the textile mills. He put all the new machines under one roof, assigned one person to each machine, and closely monitored the people as they worked arduous, twelve-hour shifts. Textile production shot through the roof. Arkwright called the enterprise a "factory." His innovation soon became the standard successful model for business, and it spread rapidly throughout Europe and America.

In his fascinating account of the daily lives of Americans during this period of great transformation, historian Jack Larkin writes: "In the years just after the [American] revolution, some Americans were already experiencing change in the routines and circumstances of their work. In the decades that followed, ever-increasing numbers would find that their daily tasks had been in some way transformed. New factories and expanded workshops were signs that, in a shift that would take generations to complete, the traditional identification of household and workplace was beginning to break apart." No longer would most Americans live and work independently in their own homes and on their own farms.

The Corporate Revolution

A second Industrial Revolution, which we will call the Corporate Revolution, took place about 100 years after the first, around the year 1900. It was then that the *corporation* was born and became the new model of business for the twentieth century. Its impact on all aspects of society and culture—both in America and around the world—has been extensive and powerful. At the heart of the Corporate Revolution were two components working in tandem that made it all possible: the commercial application of new technologies and a change in the methods of distribution of goods and services. Let me show you what I mean.

THE CORPORATE REVOLUTION began to take shape in the years following the Civil War. It was the age of the millionaire entrepreneurs—men like John D. Rockefeller, Andrew Carnegie, and Cornelius Vanderbilt. The booming telegraph and railroad industries led the way by creating huge companies with vast wealth and influence. Other industries—centered around oil, steel, chemical, and auto manufacturing—quickly followed suit by building massive companies the likes of which had never been seen.

Known more commonly at the time as "trusts," these great giants of industry virtually invented the bureaucratic system—multitudes of employees, with each person assigned to a specific department and job, all arranged in an immense, pyramid-shaped hierarchy. The bureaucratic system was so effective in the business world that it was soon adopted by the government as the best way to organize workers.

THE CORPORATIONS CREATED the "white-collar worker"—a new middle class of clerical staff (most of whom were young women), salesmen, managers, and executives. By 1900 the idea of a "profession" was becoming well-entrenched in the mindset of American society. A social contract evolved between employees and the corporations they worked for. We could call it the "Job for Life" contract: As long as you showed up on time and did the work that was expected of you, you could work for the same company until you retired. As author Michael Hammer has written: "The old social contract between companies and employees traded obedience for a stable job, but taxed the transaction with routine and boredom." By the 1920s, thanks to steady jobs and the prosperity of big companies, people were beginning to aspire to something called the "American standard of living"—later referred to as the "American dream."

Despite the urbanization that began in the Industrial Revolution, the vast majority of Americans in the 1880s still lived in rural areas and worked in farming and food production. But thanks to the Corporate Revolution, by the middle of the twentieth century, nearly seven out of every ten Americans were in some way working for a corporation or big company. Determining your own future by owning your own business, farm, or craftshop—which had been the standard for generations—became much less common in America. And the authority of corporations in people's personal lives became commonplace. Throughout the twentieth century the United States became a land of *employees,* whose lives were in far-reaching ways influenced and directed by the companies they worked for.

THE CORPORATE STYLE of business in 1900 evolved directly from Arkwright's factory model of the Industrial Revolution in 1800. Remember, Arkwright's idea was to control the workers in the textile mills, watch over them, and make sure that they stayed hard at work at their tasks. Workers were assigned specific tasks that they performed over and over again. Labor was paced and guided by the clock, not by the natural rhythms of the seasons, as it had been for centuries. When the clock said it was time to work, well, then, that's what you did or you were let go. If the boss said you had to work twelve hours a day, that's what you did. The mega-companies that cropped up in the late 1800s and early 1900s used the same approach—they just expanded the idea to include additional employees supervising other employees working even more machines.

IN THE LAST twenty-five years of the 1800s, a flood of new inventions appeared: the typewriter, the sewing machine, the telephone, the phonograph, the internal combustion engine, the motorcar, the bicycle, an incandescent electric light, electric street railways, the cash register, the adding machine, and Marconi's wireless telegraph, just to name a few.

Companies, especially in America, rushed to take advantage of the new technologies. The era of the business machine was born. The signature office machine of the Corporate Revolution was the typewriter, which absolutely revolutionized the way that business was done. Throughout the 1800s, companies had manually processed information and paperwork with the aid of rooms full of young men—working in what were called "clearing houses"—filling out forms in longhand with ink-dipped pens. But with typewriters, most of them "manned" by single young women, companies could do a lot more work in a fraction of the time. The office became a factory of deskworkers—employees working at machines for long hours, under the constant supervision and authority of a manager.

BUT THAT'S JUST half the story. The corporation not only revolutionized America by inventing the bureaucracy system, by controlling workers' lives, and by its widespread use of new technologies. A significant transformation also occurred in the way that goods were distributed to consumers.

Thanks to the Industrial Revolution, Americans created a marketplace of mass-produced goods. A localized, mercantile network of shop owners and country stores grew up in the 1800s to distribute those products around the country. But as the corporations became more powerful, they began to circumvent these traditional distribution networks in favor of a more centralized, direct approach to consumers. In the process they built a true national economy where there had once been only loosely bound regional networks. The manufacturers effectively seized control over distribution from local merchants. Just how did they do it?

Our very success as a species on this earth, and as children of our Creator, relies on our individual willingness to adapt, to innovate, to explore, to try, and to reach beyond that which we believe to be our limits. This is certainly one of history's greatest teachings.

The course of civilization has been altered again and again by those *individuals* who paid close attention to what went in the world around them—whether they were Chinese craftsmen experimenting with iron, medieval farmers watching waterwheels turn, or Renaissance printers who fine-tuned a new way of communicating.

For one thing, they created their own trained and motivated salesforces—men who traveled the country establishing and servicing accounts. The young salesmen bypassed the traditional merchants and company agents, and built completely new routes of distribution for their products. The corporations, led by the Singer Sewing Machine Company in the 1880s, also created franchising as a way to exert more command over the distribution of their products. And catalog sales and direct-mail ordering became popular, especially in rural areas. By 1900, the old system of distribution controlled by local merchants had crumbled.

Historian Olivier Zunz has written a well-researched and captivating study of this period entitled *Making America Corporate*. Zunz writes: "[The Corporate Revolution] required no less than a complete overhaul of the ways in which a society produced and exchange goods. Corporations became not only the dominant economic force of the 20th century but also a crucial element in social change, for organizations, especially pervasive and successful ones, have powerful sociological and ideological consequences."

Five More Lessons from History

HISTORY HAS A lot to teach us. The Industrial and Corporate Revolutions offer us five more lessons that help us understand the current Internet Era.

6. **The Revolution Is Everywhere**—Both the Industrial and Corporate Revolutions began in the workplace, focused around commerce. Yet the results of those changes had profound effects on society as a whole. They altered not only the way that people worked but also the way we lived, dressed, communicated, interacted, and went about our daily lives. The Internet Revolution will be just as pervasive, affecting all aspects of our society in the next few decades, sometimes in good ways and sometimes not so good. But you can bank on it that society will be completely transformed by the middle of the twenty-first century—and that the driving force behind that change will be commercial applications of Internet technology.

7. **It's Not About the Machine**—The Great Transformation that took place during the Industrial Revolution was not about new textile-spinning machines or even the steam engine. It was much bigger

than that. Likewise, the Corporate Revolution was not about the typewriter or the telephone. The effects of both movements went far beyond the capabilities of the machines that made change possible. If there is one thing most people do not yet understand about the Information Age, it is this: The Internet Revolution is not about computers; nor is it about scanners, printers, beepers, or cell phones. In the end, the Industrial, Corporate, and Information Age revolutions are *social* revolutions—they are about *people*—for they represent times of great change in our society and our culture.

8. **Technology Begets Technology**—Author and physiologist Jared Diamond wrote in his Pulitzer Prize–winning study of the history of technology, *Guns, Germs, and Steel:* "Technology's history exemplifies what is termed an autocatalytic process; that is, one that speeds up at a rate that increases with time, because the process catalyzes itself. The explosion of technology since the Industrial Revolution impresses us today, but the medieval explosion was equally impressive compared with that of the Bronze Age, which in turn dwarfed that of the Upper Paleolithic." For those of us living through the Internet Revolution, this means that new technologies will come faster, will be more rapidly accepted by society, and will bring change even quicker than ever before. By the year 2050, the 1990s will seem just as foreign and faraway as the year 1800 seems to us today.

9. **New-Found Wealth Is Part of the Package**—If one undeniable fact stands out regarding the various Industrial and Commercial Revolutions, it is that fortunes were there to be made. Consider that in the year 1840, there were only about 20 millionaires in the United States. As the Corporate Revolution began to take shape in 1879, there were 100. But by 1892, just over ten years later, there were over 4,000 millionaires in America. The historical lesson is clear: in times of great change, when emerging technologies are combined with new ways of doing business, people get wealthy.

The ecommerce age that is just beginning—this dawning era of the Internet—represents the third Great Shift in Commerce in American history. First came the Industrial Revolution of the late 1700s, and then the Corporate Revolution of the late 1800s. Both of these periods witnessed dramatic developments in technology and commerce that transformed society and created the modern world.

10. **The Secret Formula**—If we look closely at what really got the Industrial and Corporate Revolutions going and made them powerful agents for social change, we find a common formula: Emerging technologies were combined with new ways of doing business. In the Industrial Era, it was Arkwright's factory system, which relied on new textile machines,

that transformed commerce and led to mass production. The Corporate Revolution was generated by a bureaucratic business model combined with new modes of distribution (direct sales, franchising, mail order), which in turn made extensive use of the first generation of office machines.

That's one of the many reasons why Quixtar is so exciting. Quixtar's founders and business leaders have put together a totally unprecedented model of commerce designed specifically for Internet technology. Most other ecommerce sites rely on traditional mail-order and retail techniques. But Quixtar stands alone—at the vanguard of the Internet Revolution. Quixtar takes advantage of these great lessons of history and puts them to work for entrepreneurs and their families.

You Are Here

THE INTERNET REVOLUTION is the Great Transformation of our time. Can we expect the commercial applications of the Internet to have as dramatic an impact on society as the Industrial and Corporate Revolutions had? You bet. No doubt about it. As a matter of fact, because of the nature of the technology—a global network of *communication*—it's likely that the Internet Age will have an even *greater* impact on society and culture than did any of the previous Industrial Revolutions. Over the next few decades our society will be transformed and reshaped in every way possible by the uses of the Internet. This is an exciting time.

TEN LESSONS FROM HISTORY
FOR UNDERSTANDING
THE INTERNET REVOLUTION

1. **Change Happens**—The many applications of the Internet to our daily lives represent a profound turning point in human society.

2. **You Matter. Yes, You!**—History emphatically teaches us that *individual men and women do matter*. Yes, one person *can* change the world. Don't be intimidated by the new technologies. You—yes, you—could very well be one of the next great leaders of the Internet Revolution.

3. **Technology Gets Around**—Internet technology will one day encompass all of human civilization. And Quixtar, which today only covers North America, will one day reach the entire world.

4. **The Secret Is in the Network**—A single computer is not enough in itself to transform society and usher in a new age. That only became possible when computers were *networked* together, beginning in the 1970s, creating the Internet.

5. **Commerce Is the Key**—Networking computers on the Internet may be the secret to innovation. But ecommerce will be the key that unlocks the true promise this technology offers our world.

6. **The Revolution Is Pervasive**—You can bank on the fact that society will be completely transformed by the middle

of the twenty-first century—and that the driving force behind that change will be commercial applications of Internet technology.

7. **It's Not About the Machine**—The Ecommerce Revolution is not about computers; it's about people, their families, their hopes and dreams; it's about the relationships we have with one another.

8. **Technology Begets Technology**—By the year 2050, the 1990s will seem just as foreign and faraway as the 1800s seem to us today.

9. **New-Found Wealth Is Part of the Package**—In times of great change, when emerging technologies are combined with new ways of doing business, people get wealthy.

10. **The Secret Formula**—At the heart of the great Industrial Revolutions of history are innovative business models that take advantage of new technologies.

JODY VICTOR IS a widely-acclaimed Quixtar leader, teacher, and entrepreneur. Jody's mother and father, Joe and Helyne Victor, started working with Rich DeVos and Jay Van Andel in the Nutrilite business in 1951 and were integral to the founding of the American Way Association in 1959. Following his father's example, Jody was an essential member of the team that created Quixtar. Jody and his wife, Kathy, lead an organization of business owners from around the world.

Q. Jody, you've personally witnessed a remarkable evolution in the history of business. If you had to pick one aspect about the Quixtar model that you think people really need to understand most, what would that be?

A. "That's easy. It's the one thing most people just don't get. The sociology of our business is bottom up, not top down. It hard for people, especially journalists and those who've never been directly involved, to understand this business model. Most people think that any business that does well operates from the top down. But that's not how we do things. The number one priority for anyone in a business powered by Quixtar is the newest registrant—the brand new IBO. Our success is their success. So we work from the bottom up.

"In Akron, Ohio, we had a company called Goodyear. They built a community called Goodyear Heights. They had a bank called Goodyear Bank. That

was really a top-down business model. If your foreman didn't like you and fired you, you were going to
lose your house. Your whole world was that company
and you were just a number. Most people today work
in a pyramid system for a corporation. They're just a
number in a cubicle in a department in a division.
There's always someone above you who makes more
money and has more control—all the way up to one
boss or CEO who makes all the big bucks.

"You don't always get ahead in a pyramid system
by working harder. Most of the time, it doesn't matter at all how hard you've worked. As a matter of fact,
most people would probably tell you not to work so
hard because you're making them look bad. And the
guy above you probably thinks you want his job. But
the only way you get ahead is to put somebody out of
a job and take their place. That's the pyramid model
that most of corporate America lives by.

"Our business model has always been based on a
ladder concept. You *can* get ahead by working harder.
Your promotion is based solely on your own efforts,
not on the whims of some boss you don't even like.
And people are constantly encouraging you to succeed.
With our way of doing business, you don't put someone out by moving ahead. We all move up together."

Q. And now you've tied that model into Internet technology and raised it to a whole new level of significance.

A. "Right, exactly. Our high-tech, high-touch approach
is the model for a successful business in the new

economy. People won't be able to hide behind the corporate skirt anymore. It's not about the corporation anymore. It's about the individual. It's all about building teams, mentoring others, serving others. It's about personalization and relationships. It's about family and trust. It's about believing and achieving. With our opportunity, you're going to see live rooms, not chat rooms. We're going to be filling the largest coliseums throughout the United States and Canada.

"The new technology is terrific, and we're really going to benefit in many ways from the Internet. That is what makes a lot of this possible. But it's the high-touch part of the business, the relationships that bring these teams together, that will make this business model far exceed the expectations of the experts. I have no doubt that over the next few years we will watch traditional business models and conventional approaches to marketing disappear. May they rest in peace.

I believe the businesses powered by Quixtar will collectively become the largest marketing organization in the entire world. I think that is a foregone conclusion.

"People are coming to the Web in droves. They're fascinated by it. They want convenience. They see it as a way to improve their lives, to take control. They're tired of people telling them how it's going to be and what they can and can't do in their lives. People are just sick and tired of the limited options.

They're coming to the Web to find opportunities
that don't exist anywhere else—new options, new
business models, new futures."

Q. You say "new futures." This really is a forward-thinking
business venture, isn't it?

A. "We're making decisions today that will affect children not yet born. That gets the hair to stand up on
my arm. I've seen it in my own life. My kids have
choices and options in their lives that are a direct result of the hard work that my dad did years ago—all
the miles he drove and the people he talked to. His
finished product was our raw material.

"This is an opportunity for people to have a dynamic view of their future, not a home-to-work,
work-to-home, plan-A kind of life. This gives people
options. This is a plan-B approach to business, and
we're looking at multiple options that people can
choose from. When you look at a plan-A, 9-to-5 life
versus this plan-B, living, growing, wealth-building
experience—there's no comparison.

"Anyone can cast this off and say, 'I know all about
that.' There will always be people like that. But the
people who seek the information and gain the knowledge, and who aren't lazy, that's who I want to work
with. That's who I want to hang out with. That's who
I want to help."

Q. When you look to the future, how do you see all of
this playing out?

A. "I believe the businesses powered by Quixtar will collectively become the largest marketing organization in the entire world. I think that is a foregone conclusion. But more important, I think of the kid who will one day turn to his grandfather and ask: 'Grandpa, where were you during the Internet Revolution?' What's the answer going to be? 'I didn't know it was going on?' Not a chance.

"What we are doing is eliminating the guesswork for people and opening the door to anyone who wants to reap the rewards of this information revolution. You don't have to know how to write computer code. You don't have to be polished. We know what works. We're very focused. We know how to get the job done. So that when that kid asks, 'Grandpa, where were you in the Internet Revolution?' he can answer: 'I was right there in the thick of it. I helped make it happen.'"

CHAPTER TWO

A Short History
of Computers:
In Ten Easy Steps

LISON AND I recently watched *The Wizard of Oz* on video. It ranks way up there on my list of all-time favorite films. Even though I've probably seen it at least a dozen times, it's one of those things that gets better with age. One of the best scenes in the movie is when Dorothy and her pals return to Oz, having melted the witch and taken the broomstick. Remember that part?

They stand shaking before the great, monstrous face of the Wizard, as he booms and roars. The Wizard tries to give them the brush-off. "Come to see me tomorrow," he yells. But then Toto comes to the rescue and discovers the real Wizard behind a curtain—just a man pulling on levers and shouting into a microphone. I love that scene.

Then Dorothy, the Scarecrow, the Lion, and the Tin Man start demanding what they've come for. "We brought you the broomstick just like you asked," they say. "So give Dorothy a way home, and give the Scarecrow a brain, the Lion some courage, and the Tin Man a heart." Do you remember the Wizard's response? He said: "You've got them. You've had them all the time."

When we were watching the movie the other night, I jumped up at that moment and paused the tape. "That's just like the Internet Revolution!" I said to Alison. "Right there! That's it!" That one scene from *The Wizard of Oz* perfectly embodies what's going on at this very moment with the Internet Revolution. And before you do anything else—before you click another mouse or download another Web page—I want you to understand what that scene from the movie has to tell us.

A LOT OF people out there are very comfortable with computers. There are millions of them, more and more every day. They use computers at work and probably have one at home, too. They have no problem jumping on and off the Internet, using search engines, and downloading files. They might even have a Web site of their own. These millions of people may not know exactly how a computer works or even how to fix one should something go wrong. But they don't have to. They know how to do what they need to do.

On the other hand, many other people out there now are absolutely clueless about computers. And there are millions of them as well. A lot of them are truly intimidated by the things. Some are scared of even sitting down in front of one and avoid it at all costs. They don't know a modem from a mouse. And they are utterly mystified by the Internet, especially. They know very little about how to make computers work for them and how these machines could make their lives better.

Back to *The Wizard of Oz:* when Dorothy and her friends went before the Wizard, they were terrified. They were intimidated, and they felt powerless—just as some people feel about computers. But when Toto pulled back the curtain, they instantly realized that a person was behind it—just someone pushing buttons. What they were afraid of didn't really even exist. It was all smoke and mirrors.

Computers and the Internet are just like that. What you might see before you, scary and intimidating, doesn't really exist. If you look a little closer, you'll realize that on the other side of the machine there is just another human being pecking away at a keyboard. Behind all of the technical wonders and the hoopla of the Internet Revolution are human beings—people who are pushing buttons, pulling levers, making things happen in the world.

Behind all of the technical wonders and the hoopla of the Internet Revolution are human beings—people who are pushing buttons, pulling levers, making things happen in the world.

Don't let that Lion inside of you stand there, shaking and shivering. Pull back the curtain. And even more important, help someone else to see that there is nothing to be afraid of. Be their Toto and show them the truth behind the smoke and mirrors. Help to demystify the new Digital Age for others.

ONE MORE IMPORTANT aspect of that scene from *The Wizard of Oz* helps explain what's going on with the Internet Revolution. Through most of the movie Dorothy was convinced that she couldn't get home; the Scarecrow truly believed he didn't have a brain; the Lion was sure that he had no courage; and the Tin Man was certain he had no heart.

What was it the Wizard said to them at the end? "You've got them. You've had them all the time." Of course, they did! And so do you. You've got everything you need to succeed in the twenty-first century. You may simply need to be reminded of it.

I'm talking to all you Scarecrows out there now: You think you don't have the brains to learn how to use a computer or surf the Internet? Listen to me: You do have the smarts. Using computers or navigating the Net isn't rocket science. It's just a matter of learning some new skills.

To all you Lions out there who have convinced yourselves that computers and the Internet are too intimidating and you don't have the courage to learn to use these new technologies: You do have the courage. You've got it. You've had it all the time. Using the Internet or clicking a mouse is nothing compared to filling out a tax form or driving through rush-hour traffic.

For all you Tin Men out there who just don't know if you have what it takes inside to help other people find their way through the Internet Revolution: You do have the heart. You've got it. You've had it all the time.

And especially for all of you Dorothys reading this, who wonder if you have the ability to get where you want to go in life: You do have the ability. You've got it. You've had it all the time. You're taking steps down your own Yellow Brick Road right now, as you educate yourself about the new world of possibilities spreading out before you.

That's one lesson I want you to tuck away and take with you as you go forward into the new Digital Age. You've got what it takes. You've got the smarts, the courage, the heart, and the ability to go and do whatever you dream of. Like the Wizard says: You've had it all the time.

KEEP THESE LESSONS of *The Wizard of Oz* in mind as you read the rest of this chapter. I firmly believe that one of the most useful things we can do to help demystify computers and the Internet is to know a little of the history behind them. These real-life stories put some faces on the world of computers for us. They also help us see how rapidly and recently all of these developments have occurred.

The revolution in marketing and business that is Quixtar.com is not taking place in a vacuum. It's part of a larger chain of developments that is dramatically changing our society. With that in mind, we're going to take a brief look at the history of computers—in ten easy steps.

THE INTERNET REVOLUTION that is reshaping business and society today had its beginnings in the Industrial Revolution two hundred years ago. I don't just mean that figuratively, in the sense that one great age of innovation lays the groundwork for another. I mean it literally: the direct roots of the Digital Age can be traced to the technological advances of the Industrial Era. The very same textile machines that helped create the factory system and mass production in the early 1800s provided the technology that was used to create the first computers. Let me show you how it happened.

Step 1: The Babbage Engine

THE SON OF an affluent English banker, Charles Babbage was born in 1791, just as the Industrial Revolution was picking up speed. Watt's steam engine and Eli Whitney's cotton gin were starting to have an impact on society. A notable mathematician and economist, Babbage is widely credited as the inventor of the first modern computing machine.

Babbage designed the machine, known as the Difference Engine, to calculate simple equations. These calculations would provide valuable information on tidal rhythms that was needed by thousands of ship navigators out riding the seas. Like most new inventions of the Industrial Age, the Difference Engine represented a major leap forward from conventional technology. For years, the standard practice for producing nautical tables had been for teams of human calculators—referred to as "computers"—to do all the addition and subtraction in their heads.

Thanks to funding from the British government, Babbage produced a prototype of his revolutionary machine in 1833. The mechanism worked well enough to demonstrate that a larger version was possible. Despite its promise, Babbage cast his Difference Engine aside just as quickly as he had taken it up. Something new had caught his attention.

Babbage's mechanical "computer" venture had produced a working prototype and attracted some support in the government. But the inventor started to envision improvements and think up additions to the machine, which led him to scrap the original project in favor of something totally new. As a result, he never built a full-scale Difference Engine himself. Other inventors would pick up his idea years later and build one.

BABBAGE INSTEAD WANTED to create something he named the Analytical Engine. Whereas the Difference Engine could do simple addition and subtraction, the Analytical Engine would be capable of processing any calculation whatsoever—similar to most hand-held electronic calculators of today.

Babbage spent many years drawing up plans, researching materials, and building small parts of the larger machine. Besides funding, one challenge stood above all else: How could he get the machine to work exactly as he wanted it to? How would the individual parts know what to do and when?

An important breakthrough came when Babbage began to study the latest textile machinery being used in factories and mills. As you learned in Chapter 1, those machines fueled the new Industrial economy. Babbage was particularly interested in the clever workings of an ingenuous loom design that had been developed in 1801 by French inventor Joseph Jacquard. The Jacquard loom used punched cards to direct the movement of the threads. Using the prepared cards to control the looms, weavers could mass-produce complicated images of flowers and leaves. That same punch-card technology was later used in music boxes and player pianos.

You think you don't have the brains to learn how to use a computer or surf the Internet? Listen to me: You do have the smarts. Using computers or navigating the Net isn't rocket science. It's just a matter of learning some new skills.

In the punch-cards of the Jacquard loom, Babbage found the answer to one of his most pressing problems: how to control the mechanisms (and thus the calculating abilities) of his Analytical Engine. Punched cards, and later, punched paper tape, proved to be the key method of "programming" the earliest computing machines. That same technology, based on an innovative weaving machine of two hundred years ago, would last well into the twentieth century—continuing to be the most effective way that engineers would program the first electronic computers.

Babbage would never live to see the results of his efforts. Though he persisted in his design work of the larger and more complex Analytical Engine, he died in 1871, never having completed either of his machines.

Step 2: Punch-Cards

BUSINESS MACHINES LIKE the typewriter and the cash register were at the heart of the Corporate Revolution of the late 1800s. But truly modern computers were still decades away.

Accounting machines, manually programmed by inserting punch-cards (the late 1800s successor to Babbage's uncompleted work) were used rather sparingly during the Corporate Revolution. They proved to be more of a curiosity than a reliable component of the modern office. The Tabulating Machine Company (TMC), incorporated in 1896, sold many of the first punch-card accounting machines. By 1911 TMC had just 100 customers—including steel mills, railroad companies, state governments, and department stores. Most business people, however—still trying to get used to the typewriter and the telephone—turned down the strange new punch-card machines. As in any era of innovation, the mainstream acceptance of new technologies took a while.

That same year, 1911, TMC was sold and became part of the Computing-Tabulating-Recording Company (CTR), which marketed the punch-card accounting machines along with shopkeepers' scales and specially engineered time clocks that were used to keep track of employee hours. A former direct salesman with the National Cash Register company, Thomas Watson, Sr., became the president of CTR in 1914.

In 1924, under Watson's leadership, CTR changed its name to International Business Machines, and a global icon was born. IBM led the way in integrating the use of punch-card accounting machines throughout the business world. Even during the Depression of the 1930s, IBM sold over three billion punch-cards a year and annually turned out 1,500 units of its Model 405 Electric Accounting Machine. Not surprisingly, IBM would also take the lead in producing the first modern computer.

Step 3: In the Attic

THE NEXT STEP in the historical chain of events that directly linked the current Digital Age with the Industrial Revolution began to unfold in 1936. Interestingly enough, it all started with a perplexed university student.

Howard Aiken, a graduate student in physics at Harvard University, was having difficulty solving a set of equations for a project he was working on. Aiken was aware of no existing machine that could handle the calculations he needed to have done. His proposal that Harvard should build such a machine was met with anything but a positive response.

In a moment that seems right out of a movie, an employee of the physics lab approached Aiken and told him that such a machine did in fact exist but that no one ever used it. Where was this machine? In the attic.

Next thing you know, Aiken was being escorted through the attic to a small table. There on the table he found an original remnant of Charles Babbage's calculating engine from the

1800s. Just a fragment of the original pieces Babbage had experimented with, the cogs and numbered wheels had been donated to Harvard by Babbage's son Henry in 1886. It was certainly not capable of calculating complicated equations. But just seeing the old, incomplete machine was enough to give Aiken the passion to fulfill the one-hundred-year-old vision.

There in a musty attic in 1936, the past became forever linked to the future. Graduate student Howard Aiken, who had never even heard of Charles Babbage before, picked up the torch of his dream of an Analytical Engine and carried it into the future. The future, he soon learned, was at IBM.

AFTER COMPLETING SOME research, Aiken took his proposal for the first fully automatic, electronic computer to IBM in December of 1937—complete with Babbage's idea that it could be programmed with Jacquard-type punched cards. Engineering on the computer began the following year, with Thomas Watson's support. After five years of work, in January of 1943 IBM began testing its Automatic Sequence Controlled Calculator—more commonly known as the Harvard Mark I, the world's first electronic computer. Like all of the earliest computers, the Mark I was a room-sized monster.

- It was 51 feet long, 8 feet tall, and 2 feet wide.
- Mark I weighed five tons.
- It was powered by a five-horsepower electric motor.
- It contained 750,000 individual parts, including countless switches and relays.
- The sound of the Mark I was described as "a roomful of ladies knitting."

- The machine was capable of three calculations per second.
- The computer was programmed by punched cards or paper tape—a technology Babbage had first seen on the 1801 Jacquard loom.

UNLIKE THE OLDER punch-card accounting machines, which had to be operated manually, the Mark I was fully automatic. It was capable of running an entire series of mathematical operations all by itself until they were completed—even if this took all day, which it sometimes did. But the Harvard Mark I wasn't exactly the blueprint for the modern computers that followed. In their fascinating account of the history of the computer industry, historians Martin Campbell-Kelly and William Aspray put it this way:

"Not only was the Harvard Mark I a technological dead end, it did not even do anything very useful in the fifteen years that it ran. The real importance of the Harvard Mark I was as an icon of the computer age—the first fully automatic computer to come into operation." It was not long, however, before the models for computers of the future appeared.

Step 4: Vacuum Tubes

THE SAME YEAR that the Harvard Mark I underwent its first tests, a U.S. Army–led project to build an electronic computer also got underway. Built to analyze ballistics data and the trajectories of flying shells, the Army computer was created by scientists at the Moore School of Electrical Engineering of the University of Pennsylvania. Two scholars, John Mauchly and John Eckert, led a team of engineers in building the Electronic Numerical Integrator and Computer (ENIAC). The massive machine was presented to the public in February of 1946 and was heralded an "electronic brain."

ENIAC was incredibly faster and more versatile than the Mark I. Its 18,000 vacuum tubes—each like an oversized, specially built light bulb—often attracted moths and bugs, which periodically got inside the computer and had to be removed. To this day, taking care of a computer's problem is referred to as "debugging." The ENIAC was a massive piece of machinery.

- It was 10 feet tall and covered 1,000 square feet of floor space.
- It weighed approximately 30 tons.
- ENIAC included 18,000 vacuum tubes (many of which got too hot, burned out, and had to be replaced on a daily basis), 70,000 resistors, 10,000 capacitors, 6,000 switches, 1,500 relays, and 300 blinking lights.
- The computer required an astounding 150 kilowatts of power.
- More complex than any electronic system that had ever been built, the ENIAC was capable of 5,000 calculations per second.
- The ENIAC still used IBM punch-cards to feed information into the machine.

WHILE THEY WERE building the ENIAC computer, Mauchly and Eckert began to see where they might make improvements on the design. With those lessons in mind, they had plans in place for a second computer even before the ENIAC was completed. The Electronic Discrete Variable Automatic Computer (EDVAC) was that second machine.

A similar computer based on the EDVAC, built at Cambridge University in England in 1949, was termed the Electronic Delay Storage Automatic Calculator (EDSAC). Both EDVAC and EDSAC were alike, in that they allowed the computer to store calculations in memory and use that information in future operations. That ability to store and access memory became a principal design characteristic on which all subsequent computers have been built.

AFTER THE SECOND World War, Mauchly and Eckert left the University of Pennsylvania and went into business for themselves. In 1946 they founded the Electronic Control Company, one of the first computer firms in the world. Now that they were not working directly with the Army, they began to take a different approach to computers. They no longer saw the giant machines merely as mathematical calculators to study ballistics. They instead viewed computers as helpful machines that could store and process any information—perfect for the business world. Their first product, built on contract for the U.S. Census Bureau, was the Universal Automatic Computer (UNIVAC).

Step 5: Business Machines

DURING THE 1950s IBM also stepped up its investment in computers, helping to make the device more of a business machine than a room-sized calculator. The computers were designed to handle payroll, track inventory, print invoices, and so on. IBM's first business computers included:

- Model 701, released in December 1952—which rented for about $16,000 per month and sold for $1 million.
- Model 702, released in September 1953—which sold for $1 million.
- Model 650, released in 1953—which rented for the low, low price of $3,250 a month and sold for about $200,000.

UNLIKE ITS MAIN competition, the gigantic, all-in-one UNIVAC, IBM's computers were separated into modular parts—big refrigerator-like boxes connected by fat wires—which could be spaced out around a room. Each part was designed so that it could fit into an elevator, which, of course, made delivery easier. That convenience, plus a handy service contract and discounts to universities, propelled IBM's computer sales past the UNIVAC for the first time in 1955. By the following year, there were 66 IBM 700-series computers in use around the country and nearly 200 on order.

About the same time, computer technicians were designing easier ways for the average computer user to "talk to," or program, these new machines. FORTRAN (short for Formula Translator) was released by IBM in 1957. FORTRAN, which was delivered as a box full of punched cards, became the computer language of choice for scientific and technical uses. COBOL (short for Common Business Oriented Language) was released about 1960 and was used predominantly by those in business and government to handle the typical, day-to-day needs of an office. FORTRAN and COBOL would continue as two of the main computer languages for the next twenty years.

Step 6: Transistors

THE INNOVATION THAT made the next significant transformation possible was IBM's computer Model 1401, which rolled off the factory floor in early 1960. The 1401 computer rented for close to $2,500 a month and was priced at $150,000. IBM sold an astounding 12,000 of them.

The great hallmark of the 1401 (besides its having a fast printer) was that it used transistors instead of vacuum tubes. The tubes had always been a bit clunky, to say the least. They burned out easily and frequently needed to be replaced. But transistors were less expensive, much smaller, more reliable, and considerably faster.

The transistor had been developed at Bell Labs in 1947, when scientists were trying to figure out a way to improve the quality of long-distance telephone calls. A transistor is simply a tiny electrical device that has the ability to cut on and off quickly like a light switch. But it can also act as an amplifier (what some techies call a "modulator"), increasing or decreasing the power running through it.

A transistor is sort of like a miniature dining room dimmer switch: It can turn the light on and off, or it can make the light brighter or dimmer. All you have to do is feed it a certain electrical impulse, and you can get the transistor to act the way you want it to.

TRANSISTORS HAVE THIS ability—to be both a switch and a modulator—because they include a natural element called a semiconductor. What's a semiconductor? Like the name implies, it's *sort of* a conductor of electricity: not quite as good as a copper wire but certainly better than a drinking glass. A semiconductor's ability to conduct electricity (in other words, to move electrons through it) falls somewhere in the middle. It's not great, but it's not bad either. It's a halfway good conductor. So we call it a *semi*conductor.

Germanium, a grayish, shiny-white element, was the first semiconducting substance used by Bell Labs in the 1940s to build a transistor. But by the late 1950s they had decided to use another cheaper, more reliable substance to make transistors: silicon. Found in quartz rocks, gray, crystal-looking silicon is an incredibly durable and reliable semiconductor. So silicon became the material of choice with which to build transistors.

In 1998 the total number of personal computers sold around the world reached nearly 93 million—that's in just one year. Thirty-six million of those were sold in the United States alone.

BECAUSE OF THEIR special ability to switch on and off or to modulate up and down, transistors were rapidly integrated into a variety of electrical devices beginning in the 1950s. The first transistor radio hit the market in 1954 and sold for a pricey $49.95. Transistors are now found in telephones, hearing aids, cameras, clocks, video games, stereos, ATMs, and smoke detectors, to name just a few of their many uses. And transistors are what made touch-tone dialing and color television possible. If I had to name just one invention that paved the way for the Internet Revolution and the Digital Age, it would be the transistor.

It was a logical move then, in 1959, for IBM to build a computer using transistors instead of the antiquated vacuum tubes. The transistors would still be able to switch on and off, like the thousands of vacuum-tube light bulbs. And they would provide all the fast-moving electrons that computers needed to "think." But they wouldn't get hot and burn out all the time. They were infinitely smaller and much less expensive. Computers have been built using silicon-based transistors ever since.

Step 7: Integrated Circuits

IN 1964 IBM released the System 360, which became the standard "mainframe" computer of choice for the next thirty years. It was faster, had a lot more memory, and used a new programming system called DOS, short for "disk operating system." The System 360 outsold all its competitors and made IBM the unrivaled leader of the industry. But it was still a massive, outrageously expensive set of machines. Fortunately, something was waiting in the wings that would soon challenge the monopoly of these huge mainframe computers.

In the early 1960s engineers started arranging tiny transistors on small, hand-held wafers of silicon. They discovered that if they arranged the transistors in different ways, they could increase the abilities of the computer. These wired connections of transistors—called integrated circuits, or "chips"—opened the door to the next great innovation in computers.

In 1965 the Maryland-based Digital Equipment Corporation used a small integrated circuit to build its eighth Programmed Data Processor, a computer that they appropriately dubbed the PDP-8. The PDP-8 was the world's first official mini-computer. With a price tag of only $18,000, the PDP-8 rapidly became one of the best selling computers in the world. Nearly 40,000 of them were sold.

Don't let the "mini" part fool you. The PDP-8 was still a big machine—it just wasn't nearly as big as the giant mainframe computers that preceded it. It could fit on a table rather than taking up an entire office. But it was still fast and very capable. Remember, this was years before a keyboard, mouse, or computer screen came along. The PDP-8 was a big box with all sorts of switches and blinking lights.

The real impact of the PDP-8 was that it demonstrated beyond a doubt that computers could be designed to be accessible to everyone. They didn't have to cost hundreds of thousands of dollars and take up a whole room. People began to realize, especially college students who had to reserve time to access a mainframe, that big corporations and government agencies shouldn't be the only ones to have a computer. The PDP-8 represented the beginning of the personalization of the computer.

Step Eight: The Microprocessor

A SPIN-OFF OF the space race, miniaturization and microelectronics were big buzz words in the 1960s. It was only a matter of time before integrated circuits, with all their transistors, were miniaturized. In November of 1971 the Intel Corporation of California released the first miniaturized chip—or "microprocessor"—the Intel 4004. Price tag: $1,000. The 4004 was touted as an entire "computer on a chip," and it could fit right in the palm of your hand.

The 4004 contained 2,300 transistors and could handle up to 60,000 calculations a second. (That sure beat the Harvard Mark I's three per second!)

In the early 1970s tiny integrated computer circuits (with all their transistors switching on and off, on and off) made cheap, hand-held calculators possible, as well as digital watches and clocks. They were also used to create the first home video game—Atari's Pong, which appeared on shelves in December 1974 for $350.

Microprocessors, the little wafers of silicon with transistor circuits woven into them, also paved the way for computers even smaller than the PDP-8.

Step Nine: The Personal Computer

THE NEXT REVOLUTION in the history of computers was launched in January of 1975 when the Altair 8800 appeared on the cover of *Popular Electronics* magazine. Appealing to only the most die-hard computer hobbyists, the Altair was a build-it-yourself minicomputer—complete with the new Intel 8800 chip—and was priced at about $400. A small box with little more than a few switches and flashing lights, the Altair was not capable of actually doing much. But the fact that it was so inexpensive meant that almost anyone could get his or her hands on a computer and play around with it. For that reason the Altair, as simple as it was, is considered to have been the first of the personal computers.

AS COMPUTER HISTORIANS Campbell-Kelly and Aspray have written about the Altair: "The limitations of the Altair 8800 created the opportunity for small-time entrepreneurs to develop add-on boards so that extra memory, conventional teletypes, and audiocassette recorders (for permanent data storage) could be added to the basic machine. Almost all of these start-up companies consisted of two or three people—mostly computer hobbyists hoping to turn their pastime to profit. A few other entrepreneurs developed software for the Altair 8800."

Two of those young Altair software entrepreneurs were childhood buddies Bill Gates and Paul Allen. Their partnership has become one of the great chapters in the history of computers.

In a nutshell, the story goes like this: Gates dropped out of Harvard, Allen left his corporate job, and they both hightailed it out to Albuquerque, New Mexico. In an office near the airport, electronics engineer Ed Roberts had set up shop and was cranking out one Altair after another. Gates and Allen struck up a deal to write some programming codes so that people could get more use out of the Altair. The duo formed Microsoft (*soft*ware for *micro*computers) and started to work programming. Their office was a room in the Sundowner Motel across the street from Roberts's office.

Their codes caught on, one software program led to another, and the rest, as they say, is history. Today Bill Gates is the wealthiest individual on the planet, with a net worth somewhere in the neighborhood of $100 billion. He is on track to become the world's first trillionaire by the year 2004—not bad for a "small-time entrepreneur."

IN THE WAKE of the Altair 8800 the personal computer industry really started to take off. In 1977 high school friends Steve Jobs and Stephen Wozniak, working out of Jobs's garage, created the Apple II. With a built-in microprocessor, a keyboard, a monitor, and slots to hold the magnetic "floppy" disks, the Apple II became the basic model for every personal computer that has followed.

Jumping into the game, IBM launched its own IBM PC (Personal Computer) in 1981. They sold two million units in less than three years. And in 1984, Apple brought out its Macintosh computer, which included a streamlined body and a "mouse" with which to control an on-screen cursor. The age of computer "clicking" had come to the masses.

Step Ten: Today

COMPUTERS ARE THE pivotal technology around which business and society are being refashioned. Since the early 1980s the personal computer and software industries have exploded, and there are no signs of the boom slowing down. Consider a few facts:

- In 1998 40 percent of all the money that businesses invested went to buy computer hardware, software, and related products.
- In 1998 the total number of personal computers sold around the world reached nearly 93 million— that's in just one year. Thirty-six million of those were sold in the United States alone.

- Industry analysts expect that an additional 100 million-plus computers will be sold in 1999—which means people buy almost as many PCs as they do color television sets.

- In 1990 only 15 percent of the households in the United States owned a computer. Today that percentage has climbed to over 50 percent.

- The Intel Corporation's Pentium III Processor is a single microchip containing an astounding 9.5 million transistors. Over the next few years, researchers predict that miniaturized silicon chips will be built with *hundreds* of millions of transistors.

- Sales of hand-held computers (like 3Com's Palm Pilot) are predicted to reach well over 13 million by the year 2001.

- The economic benefits derived from advances in computers make up 10 percent of the world's industrial economies—almost $2 trillion worldwide.

COMPUTERS HAVE CERTAINLY come a long way since Charles Babbage started wandering through textile mills and asking questions about the punch-cards on the Jacquard loom. The 200-year-old technology of the Industrial Revolution has indeed opened the door to the Digital Age. We are the fortunate inheritors of an amazing succession of progressive thinkers and brave inventors.

THERE YOU HAVE it—the history of computers in ten easy steps. That wasn't so bad, was it? Once you pull back the curtain and really look at what's behind all those amazing machines, you'll find that it's just one story after another about people—people who paid close attention to what went on in the world around them, who were driven by a vision, and who weren't afraid to work to make that dream a reality.

Think of Charles Babbage tinkering with his Analytical Engine, Howard Aiken designing the Mark I, or John Eckert changing a vacuum tube on the ENIAC. Think of the scientists at Bell Labs experimenting with silicon and transistors or of someone turning on the PDP-8 minicomputer for the first time. Think of Ed Roberts installing an Intel 8800 chip in his Altair, wondering if anyone would buy it. And think of Bill Gates and Paul Allen across the street in the Sundowner Motel writing computer codes. Think of Steve Jobs and Stephen Wozniak out in the garage, building the future. Now picture yourself—mouse in hand, surfing the Internet.

Once you pull back the curtain and really look at what's behind all those amazing machines, you'll find that it's just one story after another about people—people who paid close attention to what went on in the world around them, who were driven by a vision, and who weren't afraid to work to make that dream a reality.

The story of computers is a story about us: It's about people who aren't afraid to learn new things and experiment and try. It's about people who woke up to the fact that yes, they do have the smarts, the courage, and the heart to go out and fulfill their dreams. It's about discovering the Wizard we have inside us who emerges from behind a curtain and says: "You've got them. You've had them all the time."

A member of the Board of Independent Business Owners representing the millions-strong global network, Fred Harteis has had an enviable career as an entrepreneur and business owner. He and his wife, Linda, enjoy a celebrated, world-wide reputation as two of the most effective leaders affiliated with Quixtar.

> **Q.** Fred, there are a lot of people out there who are intimidated by computers and by the Internet. But you have found a way to demystify all of that. You are personally taking people by the hand and showing them the way into the twenty-first century.

> **A.** "One of the critical roles we have is to simplify technology, to bring things right to where people live so that anyone can understand them. We explain the steps that people need to take, one by one, so that they are not confused. But we don't just explain. We show them. True communication doesn't mean explaining something to someone. That's too one-sided. Communication is based on other people understanding what I have said in such a way that they can apply the knowledge in their own lives.
>
> "We have developed a business model that anyone can fit in with and become successful at, if they do it right. We have very simple programs that people can follow, if they are willing to learn and ready to work. People don't need to be intimidated anymore by this

technology. Not when they have one of our IBOs sitting next to them, showing them what to do."

Q. That role of mentoring and teaching is critical to the Quixtar approach to business, correct?

A. "It wouldn't work without it. It's absolutely necessary. It really gets down to the way we approach relationships. We build teams and organizations of service-oriented people—people who genuinely want to help other people. If you don't start out with the other person in mind, it's not going to work. You give more than you expect to get. You treat people as you'd like to be treated. Be of service to other people, not for what they can give to you, but because that's the right thing to do. Our approach is this: Help people accomplish their objectives; follow through with people; be there for them; help them get to wherever they want to be. It's the right thing to do. And it's what makes this business actually work. You move ahead as you help others move ahead. It's all built on solid principles to protect the individual. The more integrity you put in, the better your business will perform. This business doesn't work with hype, games, or taking advantage of someone. So your first priority is to give of yourself. It's an old formula. But in our business, it's a formula that can make you wealthy."

Q. You have served on the Board for many years, representing the millions of independent business owners around the world. So you were there when Quixtar.com was first proposed as an idea. What's been your experience watching this momentous venture take shape?

A. "It's been one of the most exciting things I've ever had the good fortune to be involved with. I have not seen another group of men and women in my whole life who are more selflessly dedicated to the gain of other people, to other people's kids; who are focused on the long-term; who are dedicated to a bright future. If you spend time with any of these leaders, you'll see what I mean. These are people of incredible vision, who are all focused on protecting the integrity of this business. It makes me very proud to be a part of that team."

Q. What is it about Quixtar.com that you believe spells success?

A. "The unselfish backing of the DeVos and Van Andel families is so important. Here we have some of the wealthiest people in America who are willing to put it all together and then invite us to join them as partners. We also have quick access to all the products and services that people need every day. And we have teams of people who are willing to latch on to this new technology and learn what they need to learn, then share that knowledge with other people. We have unlimited potential. There is just no other business that has all the elements and advantages that we have.

"People are so hungry for time these days. We can give it to them. With Quixtar, they can shop at home over the Internet and have everything sent directly to their doorstep the next day. There is no more convenient, service-oriented place on the Internet. And people are concerned about their financial future these days. They are becoming alert to the fact that their pensions and social security just won't cut it. That's why we see such a surge of people rushing to be a part of this. People want to own their own businesses and take control of their own destiny. They can do that with Quixtar, without having to mortgage their homes and work nonstop.

Quixtar can't help but become the most powerful, successful electronic commerce model of the twenty-first century. It's a done deal.

"We offer them the opportunity to leverage their time by working with a team. With all the different business activities we have—online partner stores, interactive support, virtual catalogs, member benefits, information and consulting, the virtual office—plus the compensation plan that only we have, Quixtar can't help but become the most powerful, successful electronic commerce model of the twenty-first century. It's a done deal."

Q. If you had any advice to offer someone who was just beginning to look into the Quixtar.com IBO opportunity, what would you say?

A. "I'd say get the facts. Get the facts from people who are knowledgeable. Don't rely on opinions. One of the most important lessons I have learned in business is this: When you want to know something, ask someone who knows. If I want to know how to run a dairy farm, I'm not going to ask a lawyer or a guy who owns a restaurant. I'm going to ask a dairy farmer. And I'm not going to ask someone who ran a bad dairy farm and went out of business. I'm going to ask the most successful dairy farmer I can find. I'm going to watch him work and ask his advice. You see? Because he knows what I want to know.

"It's the same thing in any business. If you want to know whether something works, find someone who's making it work and talk to that person. Every single independent business owner who affiliates with Quixtar has someone in his or her support team who is really effective. Find and talk to that person. I'm sure he or she will be happy to answer any questions you have. Second, have some faith in yourself. God blessed you with ability and talent. Use it."

Bert and Terri Gulick lead an international team of Independent Business Owners. Successful as entrepreneurs, speakers, and teachers, Bert and Terri are widely regarded as two of the very best leaders Quixtar has to offer.

Q. Bert, someone who is unfamiliar with Quixtar may want to know, What's so revolutionary about it? There are plenty of other ecommerce shopping and information sites out there. What is it about Quixtar that sets it apart from the crowd?

A. "Have you ever mentioned Amazon.com to friends, and then they go and buy a book there? Did the people at Amazon ever pay you for that referral? Did you ever mention AOL to someone else, just in conversation as a matter of reference? Did AOL ever send you a check for referring that person to its Web site? Of course not. But Quixtar will. The best communication about the Internet, despite all the high-tech equipment, is still human beings telling other human beings about the best places to go on the Web. Therefore, the concept of networking, or referral marketing, gives us the opportunity to participate in the Internet in a way that's never been done before. Quixtar makes the advantages and benefits of this new era available to all of us, and not just as a customer but as a partner, as a fellow business owner.

"What networking does for the Internet is that it gives an ecommerce business an opportunity to go from literally nothing to being one of the top sites on the Web, overnight. What does the Internet do for networking? It gets rid of all the time-consuming activities: paperwork, processing orders, delivery and distribution, handling guarantees, collecting payments, all of that. So an individual leaves the distribution business of networking and enters the referral business of ecommerce."

Q. And the way Quixtar's development program works, it's like an all-inclusive teaching system, right?

A. "Exactly. There are a lot of people out there who own a computer and still don't access the Internet. We have the opportunity to actually introduce the Internet *and* Quixtar together, at the same time, to people. We will be the global, grassroots education process that's going to bring millions of people into the twenty-first century. It's really amazing how it all comes together. We now have an incentive, a reward for actually taking the time to teach our neighbors how to get on to the Internet and add value and convenience to their lives. No other company on the Internet offers any program like this. It is truly unique."

Q. Let's talk a little about Quixtar as a business opportunity. Someone who may have been a Quixtar client or member, who has just shopped there, may think about taking the step to becoming an independent business owner.

A. "That's where Quixtar gets really exciting. It's so much more than just the Internet's premiere shopping and information site. The IBO option that Quixtar offers represents a whole new realm of possibilities. There is no other place on the Internet where an individual can step right in and directly participate in this technological revolution. The door at Quixtar is always open.

"In other words, any individual can set up a Web site, market a product, set up the ordering process, work out the online accounting, and make the deliveries. The chance of success there, in my opinion, is even more difficult than opening up a traditional brick-and-mortar retail store. But you can go and do it if you want to. There is a lot of risk involved in getting a business up and running on the Internet. Then along comes Quixtar, which says, 'Look, you don't have to build the Web site, you don't have to handle the products, or the ordering, or the accounting, or all the deliveries. We'll handle all of that for you.' It's a new paradigm."

Q. Quixtar handles all of that but still gives you the chance to benefit as if it was your personal business?

A. "Precisely, because it *is* your personal business. That's what being an IBO is all about. If you look at all of the big businesses that are up and running on the Internet today, none of them gave the public an opportunity to get involved and benefit from their success, other than through buying stock. But Quixtar stands alone. Quixtar has said that it will share a percentage of the money that comes its way with all of its IBOs. The more people you introduce to the site, the more money you can make. It's a simple formula.

"So if you're willing to work, willing to learn, willing to develop your people skills, your income is virtually unlimited. And that income will go on to your children, from what you design and create now. No one else on the Internet is offering an opportunity of this magnitude with this much promise and success behind it, and I don't believe anyone else will."

Q. One of the key components that makes success as an IBO possible are the teaching and development programs one has access to. But there's more to it than just teaching someone about running an ecommerce business. Isn't there an in-depth personal development aspect to these programs?

A. "Sure, that's vital. Major companies in this country use PDPs, Personal Development Programs, quite extensively. Experience across the board has demonstrated that if you strive to develop someone's business skills but not other parts of his or her life, there will be shortcomings. People will only achieve just so much. Mastering business skills might make someone a great employee or an office manager, but it takes more than that for a person to develop into a leader and a true entrepreneur. With Quixtar's IBO program, we are in the business of developing entrepreneurs and cultivating leaders.

"Success in life, in anything—business, sports, the arts, you name it—depends not just on gaining the right knowledge and being able to plug into the right information source, it depends on how well you make use of the right attitudes—things like integrity, loyalty, and persistence. And you don't develop integrity, persistence, or loyalty by just educating someone about business techniques. You've got to provide more than that. The way you learn a certain attitude that will make you better at business, and a better person overall, is to immerse yourself in an environment where people share those attitudes—where great value is placed on integrity, persistence, and loyalty. These qualities are not always valued in the corporate world, but with those of us who affiliate with Quixtar, they are central to what we do. Developing those attitudes and qualities are critical to the teaching and support programs that we offer our Independent Business Owners."

We will be the global, grassroots education process that's going to bring millions of people into the twenty-first century.

Q. What's the number one thing you want people to know about Quixtar?

A. "All through our lives we come across opportunities of one kind or another. But opportunity by itself is not enough. You have to be prepared for the opportunities that life brings your way. Most people pass up the opportunities they are faced with, for whatever reason. And they end up looking back one day and wishing they had taken a different path. Most people can actually look back on the exact moment in their lives when they passed up a great opportunity.

"Quixtar is launching in such a huge way, with so much publicity and so much personal contact and recommendation, that there are literally millions of people who will be made aware of the opportunities we offer. But they have to realize that *being prepared* to take advantage of those opportunities when they come up will be very important. The opportunities and rewards are there, no doubt about it. If you are prepared to work and learn, then this may just be the moment you look back on and say: That was the time you grabbed hold of a great opportunity and succeeded."

CHAPTER THREE

It's a Dot Com World:
The Internet and
Electronic Commerce

A S YOU WILL recall from Chapter 1, no innovation or invention exists by itself. It is part of a matrix of other devices and part of a human social network. Remember, the secret is in the network. Picture the waterwheels of Europe's pre-Industrial Age eight hundred years ago, all tied in with hammers, saws, and other tools. Imagine the network of Medici banks throughout Europe during the Renaissance or the network of printing presses during the Reformation. It's when innovations and inventions are networked together that they make their greatest impact on society.

We saw this same lesson in the history of computers. Remember the transistor? What a fantastic little invention that was. But it was even more amazing when engineers tied them all together in one integrated network—the silicon chip. That's when things really started to get interesting.

All of which brings us to the Internet: a global *network* of computers. It was with the advent of the Internet—especially the World Wide Web in the early '90s—that the intense,

77

revolutionary effect of computers began to be felt throughout society. Just where did the Internet come from? And what
exactly is an Internet, anyway? These questions and more are
answered in the following Internet Timeline. Enjoy.

From Sputnik to the Web: An Internet Timeline

The 1950s and 1960s: Linking the Computers

October 4, 1957—The Soviet Union launched Sputnik, the
world's first spacecraft. For three months the 184-pound satellite circled the earth at 18,000 miles an hour, over 500 miles
high in the air. Sputnik flew over the United States at least
seven times each day, setting off waves of hysteria and Cold
War paranoia.

November 3, 1957—The USSR launched Sputnik II, a satellite six times heavier than its predecessor. Sputnik II
contained a dog named Laika, who became the first living
creature in space. Laika, the "cosmodog," only survived for
about one week in the orbiting capsule.

January 7, 1958—Responding to criticism that he had let
the United States fall behind the Russians in space and missile research, President Eisenhower appealed to Congress for
funds to establish a special organization that would take the
lead in space research and high technology. That organization was named the Advanced Research Projects Agency, or
ARPA for short. Congress soon approved Eisenhower's re-
quest and granted $520 million to establish ARPA.

October 1, 1958—On this day a separate civilian agency, the National Aeronautics and Space Administration (NASA), was established to focus just on space and missile research, so that ARPA could concentrate on other high-tech subjects like computer science. What we know today as the Internet evolved from work begun by ARPA scientists and engineers. (Because ARPA reported to the Department of Defense, it was at times also referred to as DARPA, *Defense* Advanced Research Projects Agency.)

October 1, 1962—Joseph Licklider became the first director of ARPA's computer science research division. Licklider began by suggesting that ARPA look closely at the idea of networking computers together. Keep in mind that the technology already existed whereby multiple terminals could be connected to one main computer (think of a bunch of keyboards on different desks plugged into the same machine). But the big computers themselves were like islands, unable to "talk" to each other. Licklider's proposal was to build bridges that would link all those islands together.

1966—A former manager at NASA, Bob Taylor took over as head of ARPA's computer research division. Picking up on Licklider's networking ideas, Taylor secured funding for the project in February. The undertaking would come to be called the ARPAnet—the ARPA network. Contrary to what many people believe, the ARPAnet was not created as a fail-safe communications network in case of a nuclear attack. It was principally devised as a way to facilitate research, communication, and cooperation among computer scientists, engineers, and others who had access to a computer.

1967—One of the central challenges of the ARPAnet was developing a method so that different computers using different programs could "talk" to each other. The situation at the time was like a United Nations meeting of ambassadors from all around the world but with no translators. If everyone spoke a different language, how could they all communicate?

The solution, which was first proposed at an ARPA design meeting in April of 1967, was to give each computer its own "translator"—that way, the "translators" could all talk to each other in one language but could still turn and relay messages to the big mainframe computers in their own language. These little "translators" would be specially designed minicomputers, which were then still relatively new. These minicomputer "translators" were called Interface Message Processors (IMPs)—what today we call routers.

August 1968—ARPA began soliciting bids from interested companies who wanted to build the "translators," or IMPs. None of the computer heavyweights at IBM, AT&T, or the Control Data Corporation submitted a bid to get involved in the project—they all said the computer networking idea wouldn't work.

December 1968—The $1-million contract was awarded to Bolt, Beranek & Newman (BBN), a computer research company in Cambridge, Massachusetts. Engineers at BBN signed on to retrofit four minicomputers that could serve as "translators," or IMPs, and thus create the first network of computers. The four minicomputers (the translators) would then each be assigned their own mainframe computer. Those computers would be located at four universities out west: UCLA, Stanford, UC Santa Barbara, and the University of Utah—the first four "nodes" of the ARPAnet.

1969—The team at BBN in Massachusetts worked throughout the year to meet the September 1 deadline, when they had to deliver the first IMP to UCLA. The "translators" would communicate through modems (which had been around for a few years) over phone lines, using "packet switching."

Packet switching has made the Internet possible. In a nutshell, packet switching is when a computer takes a chunk of information—whether it is an e-mail message, a Web page, music, or video—breaks it down into little pieces called "packets," routes them through phone lines to their destination, and then puts all the packets back together on the other end. Sending packets, or little pieces at a time, makes it possible to fit huge amounts of information onto the phone lines, which is how many millions of people can now access the Internet at the same time.

All of which brings us to the Internet: a global *network* of computers. It was with the advent of the Internet—especially the World Wide Web in the early '90s—that the intense, revolutionary effect of computers began to be felt throughout society.

September 1, 1969—The first IMP was installed at UCLA. The ARPAnet was off and running.

October 1, 1969—The second IMP was installed at Stanford. The first message sent across the network, between UCLA and Stanford, was "LOG IN"—well, almost. The whole system crashed when they typed the G in LOG. But before the day was out, they had everything working again and messages were being sent back and forth.

November 1, 1969—The third IMP was installed at the University of California in Santa Barbara. A month later, on **December 1**, the fourth IMP was installed at the University of Utah. So by the end of the decade there were a total of four computers on the ARPAnet.

The 1970s and 1980s: Linking the Networks

March 1970—The fifth stop on the Information Superhighway was created when an IMP was installed at the BBN lab in Massachusetts—the Net had gone national.

July 1970—A method for packet switching over radio waves instead of phone lines was developed in Hawaii and named Alohanet—the first wireless network.

July 1972—Ray Tomlinson, an engineer at BBN, invented a program that made it easier to send and receive messages over the ARPAnet—and electronic mail was born. Tomlinson's use of the @ symbol to identify someone's location became a standard. Within the year, three-fourths of all traffic zooming back and forth through the Net was e-mail.

October 1972—At the International Conference on Computer Communications at the Washington, D.C., Hilton Hotel, the wonders of the ARPAnet were presented to the public for the first time.

1973—The ARPAnet went global when England and Norway were connected to the network.

1974—As networking technology spread, new networks besides the ARPAnet started to sprout up in the early '70s. But since each network had its own rules about how to organize the flow of information, they could not connect and "speak" with each other. Every network did things a little differently. The various networks were like a bunch of separate rooms with no doors connecting them. In the late '60s engineers at ARPA had solved the problem of how to get different computers to communicate—but by 1974 the challenge was getting all the new *networks* to communicate.

In May of that year, engineers Vint Cerf and Bob Kahn proposed a way to build doors between all the different networks—in fact, they called them gateways. Their gateways would link all the various networks and databases and make it possible to send and receive messages from one to the other. Cerf and Kahn called this inter-network of networks the InterNET.

January 1975—As you read in the last chapter, the personal computer industry began when the Altair 8800, a mail-order computer, appeared on the cover of *Popular Electronics* magazine.

1977—Steve Jobs and Stephen Wozniak unveiled the Apple II personal computer.

1981—IBM launched its own personal computer. Price tag: $4,500.

1982—The number of computers online surpassed 200 for the first time. With the popularity in personal computers, that number skyrocketed throughout the '80s.

January 3, 1983—*Time* magazine named the personal computer "Man of the Year" for 1982. The cover story read in part: "By itself, the personal computer is a machine with formidable capabilities for tabulating, modeling or recording. Those capabilities can be multiplied almost indefinitely by plugging it into a network of other computers. This is generally done by attaching a desk-top model to a telephone line (two-way cables and earth satellites are coming increasingly into use). One can then dial an electronic data base, which not only provides all manner of information but also collects and transmits messages: electronic mail. . . . The entire world will never be the same."

1983—Until now all the sites, or destinations, on the Internet had their own number to identify them, which was sort of like a telephone number. If you wanted to go to another site, you had to enter a long series of numbers in just the right order. It could be very confusing.

In November of 1983 a much more convenient method was developed—the Domain Name System—which allowed sites to take on a real name instead of a long series of numbers. That way you could have a site named "Quixtar Revolution," for example. To keep track of all the names, a three-letter ending was used to group them into categories. That gave us the familiar endings like .edu (for schools and universities), .gov (for government), .org (for nonprofit organizations), and, of course, .com (for commercial use).

1984—Apple introduced its Macintosh computer, the first mass-marketed computer that had a point-and-click mouse.

1985—By the mid-1980s a handful of private companies were selling dial-up service so that people could connect to the Internet with their personal computers. These early Internet Service Providers (ISPs), each of which became its own online community, were companies like Source, CompuServe, and Prodigy. In 1985 a company called Quantum began providing Internet service as well. In 1989 Quantum changed its name to America Online. Today AOL is fast approaching 20 million subscribers.

1986—By this year the National Science Foundation had funded the creation of an updated network of super computers—which was called the NSFnet. It quickly became the stronger, faster, new "backbone" upon which most of the Internet traffic traveled. By 1990 the old ARPAnet computers and their IMPs had been quietly retired.

1987—The number of computers online surpassed 10,000

1989—The number of computers online broke 100,000 for the first time. By 1992 that number would pass 1 million for the first time.

The 1990s: The Web Is Born

THE INTERNET THAT millions of people are discovering and using today did not exist at the beginning of the 1990s. Sure, it was much the same computer network—with all its routers and phone lines and packets of information zipping around. But cyberspace didn't look anything like it does now. Aside from a few specialty services, nearly everything that might come up on your computer screen back then was just text and tree-like diagrams with files tucked into folders. Unless you were an expert, it was extremely difficult to find your way around and figure out what was what. Besides, there really wasn't all that much content that might be interesting. All of that changed in the early '90s with the advent of the World Wide Web. The Web made it much easier for people who weren't computer experts to make sense out of the Internet and benefit from all it had to offer.

Even though the terms "the Web" and "the Internet" are now used interchangeably by most people, to techies they are quite different things. As you know, computer networking started out in the 1960s when the ARPAnet was created. That led to a host of other computer networks, most of which have since been tied together as one global network we call the Internet. The World Wide Web, on the other hand, was a computer program invented in the early '90s that gave the Internet the look and feel we see today.

If the technology that created the Internet has been around since about 1970, how come it took so long for businesses to take advantage of it? Why didn't we see the explosion in Internet-based commerce until the mid- to late-'90s—almost thirty years after the Internet was invented?

The short answer to that question is this: Internet-based commerce was illegal. Until 1992 individuals and companies were forbidden by federal law from making any money using the Internet.

The Web brought to the Internet all those pictures, links, windows, and icons that make being online so much fun. The Internet is great. But the Web made it user-friendly.

A native of Britain, physicist Tim Berners-Lee created the Web in 1990 while working at CERN, the European Particle Physics Laboratory in Switzerland. Berners-Lee hoped his Web program might make it easier for the CERN scientists to exchange information back and forth over the Internet. The Web program was such a success at CERN that it was sent out over the Internet for free. Within just a few years, the World Wide Web—with its signature "www"—became the accepted format that almost everyone used to experience the Internet.

ANOTHER CRITICAL DEVELOPMENT occurred in the early '90s that made the Internet more user-friendly, thus opening it up to millions of people besides computer scientists: a program called Mosaic. Created by students at the University of Illinois, Mosaic was a "browser"—basically, a way of navigating, or browsing, your way from place to place on the World Wide Web. Your browser, for example, gives you those familiar forward and back buttons. In 1994 the inventors of Mosaic went back to the drawing board, spruced it up a bit, then re-released it as the Netscape Navigator.

WITH THE WORLD WIDE WEB and browsers commonly available, hooking up to the Internet became ever more popular throughout the 1990s. Content on the Web improved and going online became a daily event for millions of people around the world.

Despite that fact, little had actually been written for the general public about using the Internet when New York librarian Jean Armour Polly wrote an article in 1992 about what it was like to go online. You may not have read her article, published in a library bulletin in June of that year. But chances are you would recognize the title: "Surfing the Internet."

Polly likened the online experience to surfing, and the Digital Age's most well-known metaphor was born. Why surfing? Well, the mousepad Polly was using at the time had on it the image of a surfer riding a big wave. That caught her attention while she was trying to think up a title—and the rest is metaphor history.

THE INTERNET HAS become the primary force shaping society and business as we move into the twenty-first century. Computers are indeed amazing—and they get more amazing and versatile all the time. But the secret of powerful innovation that impacts society is in the network, and the Internet is proving that more and more every day.

In April 1998, the U.S. Commerce Department released a report on the emerging digital economy. Perhaps the most memorable excerpt from that report reads as follows: "The Internet's pace of adoption eclipses all other technologies that preceded it. Radio was in existence thirty-eight years before fifty million people tuned in; TV took thirteen years to reach that benchmark. Sixteen years after the first PC kit came out, fifty million people were using one. Once it was opened to the general public, the Internet crossed that line in four years."

The Internet is no fad. It is well deserving of all the press, all the hoopla, and all of the hype that it has received. If anything, the Internet is not hyped enough. As I wrote at the beginning of this book, the Internet Revolution represents the great transformation of our times. And when all is said and done, networking technology will have a more profound impact on society than the Industrial and Corporate Revolutions combined.

TRACKING THE NET: THE LATEST FIGURES ON INTERNET GROWTH.

- There are already just over 100 million people online in the United States and Canada. The number of Internet users worldwide is estimated to be about 200 million.
- Researchers predict that in the year 2000 an estimated 327 million people around the world will be Internet users.
- There are well over five million Web sites, up from 26,000 in 1993.
- English is the dominant language on the Net right now. But by the year 2005, 60 percent of all the people online will speak a language other than English.
- 760 U.S. households go online every hour.
- Senior citizens are one of the fastest growing segments of the population rushing to be part of the Internet.
- 90 percent of the 112,000 schools in the United States are online, including more than a third of K–12 classrooms.
- 63 percent of adults in the United States use computers fifteen hours a week, on average—six of which are spent on the Internet.
- By the year 2002, 2 million people will be taking college courses online.

- Nearly half of those online say that high-speed Internet access is the number one thing they will look for in their next home.
- Analysts believe that by the year 2005 there will be over 77 million children and teenagers online all around the world.

Electronic Commerce

AS YOU LEARNED from the history of innovation in Chapter 1, networking new technologies is one of the most significant developments that signals a great period of dramatic change in human history. But the role played by commerce in that process is the key factor to watch. When a new technology becomes an integral part of business, it truly begins to transform not only commerce but society as well. We saw this happen with the steam engine and the new textile looms around 1800. And it happened again with telephones and typewriters around 1900. Today we are all witnesses to the dramatic effects that are unfolding as Internet-based commerce begins to power up. Perhaps the most exciting aspect of all is the fact that this great revolution is just now getting started.

Along with the invention of the World Wide Web and the Mosaic (Netscape) browser, electronic commerce has been the essential ingredient responsible for the explosive growth of the Internet since the early 1990s. I'm often asked: If the technology that created the Internet has been around since about 1970, how come it took so long for businesses to take advantage of it? Why didn't we see the explosion in Internet-based commerce until the mid- to late-'90s—almost thirty years after the Internet was invented?

The short answer to that question is this: Internet-based commerce was illegal. Until 1992 individuals and companies were forbidden by federal law from making any money using the Internet. After that ban was lifted, business leaders started to reevaluate the role that computers and the Internet could have in their ventures. Acquiring a ".com" after the name of your company has fast become one of the first steps businesses take to retool themselves for the new Digital Age.

One Person Matters

Remember the second lesson from the History of Innovation? *You Matter—Yes, You.* Individual men and women who step forward to take leadership positions in times of great change can affect the course of history. This lesson certainly rings true when we look at how the Internet became a powerful economic force. One man put the legal machinery in motion that opened the Internet to commerce—one man.

Congressman Rick Boucher, the representative of Virginia's Ninth District, was elected to the United States House of Representatives in 1982. Around 1990, when the World Wide Web was just beginning to change the face of the Internet, Boucher had a unique vantage point in Congress. He was serving on the House Commerce Committee, the House Committee on the Judiciary, and the Committee on Science and Technology. Boucher's work gave him a profound appreciation for how the Internet was shaping up to be a powerful force in our society. He had first-hand knowledge of the phenomenal growth rate of the Internet, and he was mindful of some of the privacy and legal issues it posed. But foremost in his mind was the Internet's enormous potential as a commercial marketplace.

"One of the positions in which I served then was chair of the Subcommittee on Science," said Boucher when I interviewed him for this book. "Among the agencies that we had responsibility for was the National Science Foundation, which at that time operated all the hardware that was the backbone for the Internet in the United States. It was called the NFSnet, and it was a collection of switches and routers that handled most of the Internet's traffic. As chairman of the House Science Subcommittee, I held the first congressional hearing on the Internet and Internet policy. And one of the issues that was presented to our subcommittee then by the community of people using the Internet was the need to remove the restriction against commerce.

"The National Science Foundation had a policy—called the Acceptable Use Policy—which required that the only traffic that could traverse the Internet backbone be purely educational, scientific, or research-oriented. In other words, no commercial traffic. It was simply disallowed as a matter of federal regulation. And so there could be no electronic commerce.

"In those days," Boucher continued, "this would have been in 1991 and early 1992, there was a tremendous interest on the part of many of the people putting up Web sites to get rid of that Acceptable Use Policy. But that was going to take legislation."

ON JUNE 9, 1992, Congressman Boucher submitted a bill to the U.S. House of Representatives that would alter the course of history. It was signed into law by President Bush on November 23, 1992.

"It was a very straightforward measure that repealed the old Acceptable Use Policy," he said modestly. "It said that any traffic could traverse the Internet backbone as long as it was consistent with the growth and development of the Internet. And so we permitted commercial traffic on the Internet for the first time. That was the first enactment that Congress ever passed dealing with the Internet. And it was that repeal of the Acceptable Use Policy that created the circumstances for electronic commerce on the Internet to arise."

The Internet that millions of people are discovering and using today did not exist at the beginning of the 1990s.

Boucher spelled out some of the thinking that went into the simple yet historic legislation: "Beginning in the early '90s people began to use the Internet much more rapidly than they had in the past. The growth was absolutely enormous. There were growth figures of more than 100 percent every two months. And it's still growing. It became apparent to me in those days that the government needed to get out of the way.

"For the Internet to realize its true potential, we needed to do two things: first, repeal the Acceptable Use Policy so that there could be commerce on the Internet; and then secondly, have a transition from the government to the private sector for the ownership of the backbone. And we accomplished both of those things during the years that I chaired that subcommittee. The Internet backbone was privatized, and there are now multiple backbones supporting the traffic.

And Internet commerce—well, that sure has taken off. It's really amazing if you consider everything that's happening with the Internet now. We're creating an entirely new economy, and it's revolutionizing the way we do business."

YOU COULD SAY that again. In the few short years since Boucher's bill became law, Internet-based commerce has become one of the most powerful segments of our nation's economy. Analysts believe that in the next decade the Internet could become a trillion-dollar marketplace. Without a doubt, ecommerce has become the New World of business. Companies and entrepreneurs are rushing headlong into cyberspace to take advantage of all the opportunities that that world has to offer.

FOLLOW THE MONEY:
THE LATEST FIGURES ON INTERNET-BASED ECOMMERCE

- In 1999, the top 100 ecommerce Web sites reported annual growth rates of 1,000 percent—a figure that is expected to increase.
- The Internet economy generated more than $301 billion in total revenue in 1998 and was responsible for creating 1.2 million jobs.
- By the year 2003, business-to-business ecommerce is projected to rocket from $43 billion in 1998 to $1 trillion by 2003.

- Business-to-consumer ecommerce (online shopping) is forecasted to jump from $7.8 billion in 1998 to $108 billion by 2003.
- Nearly one-third of all Internet users shop online, and that figure is also on the rise.
- Analysts estimate that the amount that companies spend to advertise on the Internet will soar from $3.2 billion in 1999 to $11.5 billion by 2003. That total could reach $22 billion by 2004—making advertising on the Internet even more popular than on the radio.
- In 1998 an estimated six million households shopped regularly online. By the year 2010 that figure is projected to reach 20 million.
- Total online revenues could exceed $1.3 trillion by 2003. Approximately 427,000 small businesses went online between 1998 and 1999. Seventy-one percent said the Internet was "essential to their success."
- From 1995 to 1998 the information technology industry, even though it accounted for only 8 percent of America's gross domestic product, accounted for 35 percent of the country's economic growth.
- Companies worldwide are expected to save over $600 billion a year by 2002, as they reduce or eliminate traditional business costs by going online.
- By the year 2002 teens will spend $1.2 billion over the Internet, and kids aged 5–12 will lay out $100 million online.
- By the year 2003 an estimated 95 percent of college students will be online and spending $4 billion a year.

Portrait of a Revolution

BUSINESS ON THE Web has expanded into all areas of the economy. Let's take a closer look at exactly how Internet ecommerce is affecting consumer-based businesses. Here's an end-of-the-millennium snapshot of a handful of industries that are facing dramatic changes as a result of the commercial uses of the World Wide Web.

Automobiles

Online and off, the car business in the United States is a $508 billion industry, with 16 million projected car sales for 1999.

According to J. D. Power & Associates, 40 percent of new car buyers say they used the Internet to help them make the purchase.

Forrester Research reports that by the year 2003, 470,000 households will buy their cars online, totaling $12 billion in sales.

After a number of online car-buying start-ups hit the Net, Ford, DaimlerChrysler, and General Motors have each aggressively jumped into the Internet ring. GM, the world's largest automobile company, announced that it was setting up an entire ecommerce division, eGM, with a budget of no less than $1 billion.

Company to keep an eye on: CarsDirect.com, which sells, leases, insures, finances, and even delivers new cars all through its exclusive online service. Other dot coms of note: carOrder, Autobytel, AutoNation, and Autoweb, among many others.

Drugstores

The dot com drugstore market is taking off even faster than did Amazon's book and music outlet—which isn't surprising when you consider the fact that Americans spend four times as much per year on drugstore products as they do on books and CDs combined.

The total drugstore market is now worth about $164 billion a year—which breaks down like this: $101 billion for prescription drugs, $16 billion for over-the-counter drugs, $36 billion a year for personal care and beauty products, and $11 billion for vitamins and alternative remedies.

The Internet has become the primary force shaping society and business as we move into the twenty-first century.

As cyberspace drugstores boom, analysts expect a nice slice of that pie to move online. According to Jupiter Communications, there will be a whopping $1.7 billion spent online each year for drugs, vitamins, and personal care products in 2003. That includes $434 million for vitamins and supplements, $706 million for personal care, $34 million for over-the-counter drugs, and $996 million for prescriptions.

In the news: drugstore.com, PlanetRx, Walgreen's, CVS, and Rite-Aid are among the many online stores trying to grab a slice of that $1.7-billion pie.

Company to watch: Quixtar. Quixtar.com is the only place on the Web that sells Nutrilite Products, one of the bestselling brand-name vitamin and mineral supplements in the world.

Quixtar is the only online ordering service that offers Artistry cosmetics, one of the most successful lines of beauty products. Quixtar's virtual shelves also include a top-quality line of household and personal care products that can't be found in any store on- or offline. All of that, combined with Quixtar's unique marketing arm and loyal customer base, make Quixtar.com a company to watch in the twenty-first century.

Books

Jupiter Communications predicts that online book sales, which accounted for just 3 percent of total Web business in 1999, will expand to 11 percent by 2002.

The powerhouse online retail giant Amazon.com has become one of the Web's greatest success stories to date. Billing itself as "Earth's Biggest Bookstore," Amazon started selling books online in June 1995 and has since branched out to include everything from toys to sporting goods to auctions.

A publicly traded company, Amazon is valued at over $20 billion, which has made its founder, Jeff Bezos (who owns roughly 42 percent of the company), incredibly wealthy. Amazon sells approximately 75 percent of the books sold online and boasts over eight million registered customers.

With its 1,000 brick-and-mortar stores, Barnes and Noble is the nation's number one traditional bookstore—and thus Amazon's chief competitor. Or so you'd think. Despite investing over $100 million in a cyberspace venture—barnesandnoble.com, now valued at less than $3 billion—the comfy, couch-filled super bookstore has yet to pose any kind of a real threat to Amazon's reign. B & N lays claim to only 15 percent of the books sold over the Internet. And even though that number is way up over years past, some analysts wonder whether the old way of selling books might be on its way out.

Fordham University business professor Albert Greco, who studies the book business, told *Wired* magazine in June of 1999 that the continued growth of online retailers "is going to be a cannibalization" of brick-and-mortar stores.

Groceries

The supermarket business is a $450-billion industry in the United States.

How much of that is going online? According to Jupiter Communications, online groceries are forecasted to become a $3.5-billion business by the year 2002—up from $350 million in 1999.

To date, a number of online supermarkets have already made a name for themselves regionally, offering Web-based shopping and home delivery: Webvan in the San Francisco area, Home Grocer in Seattle, Netgrocer in New York, and Peapod in Chicago and Boston. Also vying for business in the Boston area are ShopLink, Streamline, and HomeRuns.

Have Cart, Will Travel: Hoping to become the first nationwide online grocery store, Webvan announced in 1999 that it would build $1 billion-worth of automated distribution warehouses in cities around the country. First stop: Atlanta.

Company to keep an eye on: Quixtar—with over one million loyal shopping partners in North America and twice that number waiting in the wings around the world, plus a warehouse distribution system already in place, Quixtar has what it takes to be the first global grocery.

Real Estate

America's residential real-estate industry is a $1-trillion-a-year business.

From 1995 to 1999 the number of real-estate Web sites exploded from 3,000 to over a quarter of a million.

One study found that as many as 64 percent of home-buyers start their search online.

The nation's approximately 800,000 real-estate agents have been extremely cautious about using the Web—understandably so, because online services could likely reduce their profits or take them out of the loop altogether. Either way, their job description will definitely change in the future.

The mortgage business is a $1.5-trillion industry, less than 1 percent of which is now transacted online. But by the year 2003, analysts forecast that 25 percent of all mortgages will be handled entirely on the Web.

Most notable dot com: Realtor.com, the official Web site of the National Association of Realtors, lists well over 1 million homes online.

Banking and Financial Management

The number of U.S. households that go online to do their banking is expected to increase five-fold in the next few years: from about 8 million at the end of 1998 to 40 million by 2004.

Nearly 14 million U.S. households will pay their bills online by 2004.

According to the U.S. General Accounting Office, the number of banks, thrifts, and credit unions online grew from just one in December 1995 to 2,100 by June of 1999.

By 2003, 86 percent of banks will offer online services, covering everything from account management to loan approval to discount brokerage.

Analysts believe that in the next decade the Internet could become a trillion-dollar marketplace. Without a doubt, ecommerce has become the New World of business. Companies and entrepreneurs are rushing headlong into cyberspace to take advantage of all the opportunities that that world has to offer.

Company to watch: PaceFinancial.com—a Virginia-based start-up that offers all-in-one investment and portfolio management, plus expert advice with a unique, streamlined, user-friendly platform.

Stocks and Investing

According to a June 1999 study by Gomez Advisors and the polling firm Harris Interactive, online investing has become a mainstream activity. There are now over 5.1 million online investors, representing 11.2 million accounts. The number of online investors could swell to nearly 20 million in the next few years, increasing the industry's assets by $1.1 trillion.

The number of companies offering online trading and investing went from 24 in 1997 to 140 by 1999.

Web investing has also opened the door to a boom in day trading—the buying and selling of a high volume of stocks online, in hopes of earning profits on the daily fluctuations of the market.

New wonders: Wireless trading, which allows people to buy and sell stocks using pagers and mobile phones.

Buying and selling: Schwab handles 28 percent of all Web trades, making it the top broker in cyberspace. But not far behind is E*Trade, with 14 percent and climbing. Also in the ring: Ameritrade, Datek, DLJ Direct, and Merrill Lynch, among others.

WE MAY REFER to it as the *virtual* world, but cyberspace business is anything but virtual. It involves real money, real wealth, real opportunity, and real change. In addition to the few industries we looked at here, countless other businesses will be affected by the Internet over the coming years. Some will be slightly modified. Others will be totally overhauled. And a few will be devastated.

"It's a dot com world," says David Millican, an investment broker with A. G. Edwards in Atlanta. "That's the name of the game. I don't care who you are or what your business is. If you don't have a strategy that involves the Internet in some way, then you're kidding yourself. You can't ignore it. The Web is here to stay."

Author, entertainer, and entrepreneur, Andy Andrews is quite well-known even outside the Quixtar business world. As a professional comedian, Andy has appeared on premiere stages in Las Vegas and Atlantic City, has been seen countless times on television, and has even performed for the Reagan and Bush White Houses. As Quixtar leaders with a global business, he and his wife, Polly, travel extensively, offering their experience and knowledge to Quixtar's hundreds of thousands of independent business owners.

Q. Andy, what is it that makes Quixtar stand out from the crowd of other ecommerce sites on the Web?

A. "A lot of companies are just now coming to the Internet to try and figure out the new economy. And one of the things they don't like is that there is no loyalty anywhere. Amazon.com is one of the most widely known shopping sites. But even the Amazon folks can't figure out the loyalty issue. You might buy a book from Amazon one week, and the next week buy it from Barnes and Noble, and the next week at your local bookstore, and the next week at the airport. What do you care? It makes no difference to you where you buy your book.

"But with Quixtar you're not just a faceless customer on the Web, you're a partner. You're an independent business owner, and your success is Quixtar's success. We're all working together. It's your store, your Web site. You get a piece of everything you buy. You get a piece of everything you refer. And this is just like being loyal to any other business you own. If you own a McDonald's, you don't go out to lunch at Burger King. A Mercedes is a great car. But

if you own a Jaguar dealership, you're not going to buy a Mercedes. You're loyal to your own store, your own business.

For the first time in history, people can go on the Internet and link to Quixtar and make one decision that will allow them to make all the other decisions in their lives.

"So this has solved the ecommerce loyalty issue for so many companies. Rather than going to the trouble of creating their own Web site and paying a fortune for advertising, all they do is partner with us. I read somewhere that Amazon.com spent $60 million on advertising. And that's to attract a base of buyers who are not even loyal to their products. Quixtar has solved the expensive advertising issue and the loyalty factor on the Web. All companies have to do is partner with us, and we offer them a loyalty that can't be beat anywhere else on the Internet. There is nothing else like this on the Internet, nothing. And there isn't going to be, because there isn't a company in the entire world that can bring millions of loyal partners to the table. Quixtar is completely unique."

Q. What do you see as the role of the teaching and support programs that Quixtar IBOs make use of in building their businesses? You hear the word *duplication* used once in awhile in connection with them. What's that all about?

A. "People think that when we talk about duplication, we're talking about making exact replicas of ideas or people, like a cookie cutter. Like, you have to look and think just like me if you want to be successful. That's really funny. But that's not the form of duplication that makes Quixtar the stickiest Web site on the Internet. What most people don't understand is that building this type of a referral business, just like building a string of McDonald's around the world, requires a proven formula that anybody can apply and benefit from. It's a reliable business model that's being duplicated.

"Look at it this way. You could be the smartest person in the world, and you could be the easiest person to relate to in the world. But there's only one of you to teach those attitudes and skills to your team. So if you're not plugging people into a learning and development program, then you will be the only one who knows how to do anything. You will be the only one who knows how to explain Quixtar and ecommerce. You will be the only one who knows how to explain our referral-based compensation package. If there's not something bigger than you helping you teach and inform and motivate, then you will be all alone. And if you are the only leader, then you are indispensable to your business and you can't leave.

You're a slave to that business. Your business owns you. With Quixtar, it is the business development program that's indispensable, not you all by yourself.

"We're duplicating a proven business method, a marketing model, just like McDonald's duplicates its business model. These programs provide this training and information to everyone equally, whether you are a brand new IBO or you have been around for years. It's impossible to build a group of people and hold them together in a reliable web of communication without having that development program in place that teaches and informs everyone in the network."

Q. Sometimes you hear Quixtar IBOs talking about freedom, and "making the decision to be free." Can you explain that?

A. "A lot of people have a hard time making a decision. I used to think a lot of people had a hard time saying yes. And then I thought a lot of people had a hard time saying no. But now I realize people have a hard time saying anything. Through the years, people have gotten used to not making their own decisions.

"We actually live in a country where most of the people have someone else decide what time they go to bed; because someone else decided what time they have to get up; and what time they have to be at work; and what they will do when they get there; and what time in the day they will drink coffee; and somebody else decided how long they will have to stand there and drink it. And for most of the adult men and women in America, somebody else decides when they can eat lunch, where they can go, and what they can afford to eat when they get there. And somebody else decides for them where they can go on vacation and how long they can be gone.

"Somebody else decides when they can go home at the end of the day and how much time they will have to spend with their families. And someone else even decides how often they can be sick. This is all because once upon a time, maybe many years ago, someone sat down and looked at a piece of paper and decided how much they were worth and how much income they would make. And people took it and gave up their right to make decisions about their own lives. So they went to work for that amount and they sold their lives, one hour at a time, one paycheck at a time.

"This was an insidious little thing that happened all across America throughout the twentieth century. And now we've got millions of people who are used to this and actually think this is normal. But it's not normal. It's a form of slavery. With Quixtar's IBO option, that doesn't have to happen to anyone else ever again. The key is to actually make a decision, to make the decision that you won't put up with this anymore. For the first time in history, people can go on the Internet and link to Quixtar and make one decision that will allow them to make all the other decisions in their lives."

A member of the influential Independent Business Owners Association, Jim Floor was one of the key players involved in the creation of Quixtar. He and his wife, Margee, are two of the most renowned and highly regarded business leaders affiliated with Quixtar.

Q. Jim, what is it about Quixtar that you believe is so promising?

A. "I think we have a sure thing for two basic reasons. Number one, I believe that the electronic commerce marketplace will take shape with or without Quixtar, with or without you or me or anybody else. This emerging multi-trillion dollar marketplace is going to happen, period. And I think it will lead to the greatest transfer of wealth in our history. Over the next ten years or so, the Internet Revolution will change everything about how we live.

"The key to the new online marketplace, however, is developing people's loyalty to buying on the Internet. And the competition is fierce to get customers. Right now, the competition is focusing on two elements: advertising and price. But the best move of all would be to put a profit motive into the picture so that people are compensated to go to a particular Web site. That's where Quixtar comes in."

Q. Quixtar literally pays people to shop from its Web site?

A. "Right, and they will pay quite well. I've heard that an ecommerce site is like a store in the desert with no road map to get there. There are so many of them being put on the Internet that unless people have a specific reason to go to them, they'll just wander around like they're in a desert. And it's hard to know for sure if you're getting the best deal. There's no loyalty anywhere and no telling that you'll take the same route twice. When you add the financial incentive that Quixtar offers through its layered compensation package, you add a whole new understanding of loyalty. The loyalty is built in to the experience. Quixtar combines what is best about the new Internet marketplace with a one-of-a-kind loyalty program."

Q. One of Quixtar's primary advantages is that it offers a high-touch experience to an otherwise impersonal medium, the Internet. Quixtar literally brings people together *off-line.*

A. "You bet. We're essentially taking advantage of three market trends in order to make this happen. Number one is the power of duplication, which for decades now has been used in the franchise industry as the way to do business and minimize risks. We're also taking advantage of the growth in home-based businesses, which is shaping up to be the way that a great deal of business will be conducted in the twenty-first century. And we're taking advantage of the exploding new ecommerce marketplace that is just now emerging.

"But none of them by themselves, though, adds the high-touch aspect. That has to come from person-to-person, one-on-one contact or from a small group meeting. That puts the human touch back into this highly technical industry. These online shopping communities don't build themselves. You will either have to spend a large fortune, most of your income, on advertising; or you will have to compensate people for word-of-mouth referrals. We prefer the human touch. It's an important point, because those people who think technology will replace the human touch will never succeed in this business.

"What's the glue that will hold these online communities together? It's not the best price, because that can always change. It's not the most convenient delivery system or the best service; all of those are merely enhancements. The glue that keeps this community growing is the interaction you have with other human beings, the encouragement, and one-on-one exchanges. It's about meeting new people and sharing in the lives of others. That can never be replaced by a computer, by e-mail, or by any technology. It's the people who bring the business together and make things happen. Without them, you don't have a business."

Q. Quixtar has been heralded as the great new model of business for the Internet era. But in its purest form, when you get right down to it, isn't Quixtar still about an opportunity?

A. "No question about it. You know, the number one dream in America for many years was home owner- ship. But in the past twelve months that dream has moved to number two. The number one dream people have today is to spend more time with their families. And that's because as a society we have come to a place where, for the most part, we are enjoying an incredible lifestyle. But we're finding that nice cars, and nice clothes, and bigger homes, and more vaca- tions don't provide the kind of happiness and real life significance that we seek to be happy and fulfilled. It's our families and our extended families and the people we care for who add value to our life.

"But the problem is, we are so busy. We run so hard from the time that alarm clock goes off until our head hits the pillow that we rarely spend any quality time with our families. I read a survey recently that

> It's the people who bring the business together and make things happen. Without them, you don't have a business.

says the average father in America today spends two hours a day watching television, which is basically his way of zoning out, and only five minutes a day in personal, one-on-one communication with his children. He's so burned out mentally, and so burned out physically, that he'd rather sit alone in front of an idiot box and let it entertain him than to say to his son or daughter, 'Let's go do something together. Let's just talk.'

"I think the number one dream in America today is to get off the treadmill everyone is running on. But at the same time, most Americans aren't willing to give up the lifestyle. So the question becomes, how do you do both? And people are looking. They're buying lottery tickets and trying to play the stock market. They're out there trying to gain the wealth that will buy that freedom without sacrificing the lifestyle. On the other hand, a lot of people are paring down their lifestyle, settling for less as a way to try and get their life under control.

"Quixtar is a unique business model tied into the latest technology that gives people the *opportunity* to be able to purchase their freedom back without sacrificing their lifestyle—and in the process, enhancing their own personal growth and finding out that they're more capable of doing things than they realized. All of a sudden they get excited not only about their own freedom but also about what they can accomplish and the significance they can have in other people's lives."

Q. What's the number one thing you want people to know about Quixtar?

A. "The vast majority of people with whom I have worked over the last twenty years have undersold themselves. They are capable of far greater things than they ever realized. And the mindset that it takes for someone to discover his or her abilities, the genius that lies within, is a minor mental adjustment. Ultimately, only a minor adjustment will move people from thinking that they can just barely get by to believing they can excel in all areas of their lives.

"The message that I would like people to get first about Quixtar, before they understand anything else, is that they already have a spark of genius within them; a spark that, properly recognized and properly utilized, can lead them to the lifestyle of their dreams and an opportunity to make a significant contribution to the lives of people they care for."

PART TWO

HIGH TOUCH

CHAPTER FOUR

The Historic Roots
of Quixtar.com

I N   T H E   F I R S T part of this book we put the current
Internet Revolution into a broader historical context and
saw it as just the latest in a long chain of innovations and
changes. It is indeed an exciting time. The next few decades
will be a period of great transition and opportunity, as the
expansion of the Internet into our daily lives proves to be a
seismic event in human history.

As we learned, the commercial applications of emerging
technologies are often the driving force behind these great
transformations. Enter Quixtar.com.

One of the most impressive ventures to hit the Internet,
Quixtar leads the way across the threshold to this new era.
Quixtar.com promises to be a major player in the new world
of ecommerce. Versatile, progressive, and full of opportunity,
Quixtar represents the Internet and ecommerce at their best.

Quixtar is the perfect symbol of this new age of innovation, which will reshape our world in the twenty-first
century. Like no other company on or off the Internet,

Quixtar skillfully weaves together new technologies in a way that greatly improves our lives. But even more important, Quixtar gives each of us the opportunity—no matter what our background, gender, income, or education—to play a leadership role in the Internet Revolution. With the perfect mix of high-tech and high-touch, there is no other business venture quite like it. Quixtar.com stands alone.

In this chapter, we are going to take a look at the historic roots of Quixtar.com. Quixtar grew out of two twentieth-century business phenomena: referral-based marketing and ecommerce. Both of these revolutionary approaches to business are brought together as never before under this totally new paradigm. In the last chapter, we considered the development of electronic commerce. Now we will explore the evolution of referral-based marketing.

The Origins of Referral-Based Marketing

LET'S TAKE A quick look at how the referral-based marketing business model evolved. Just where did it come from? Referral marketing grew out of the union of two revolutionary approaches to business and product distribution, both of which originated in the Corporate Revolution of the late 1800s: franchising and direct sales.

Franchising

Like direct sales, franchising was an innovative way of distributing goods and services that emerged along with new technologies in the late 1800s. The word *franchise* is derived from the French and originally meant "to free from slavery or servitude." Isaac Merritt Singer, inventor of the Singer sewing machine, is most often credited for having created franchising. Singer, a forty-year-old U.S. actor-turned-inventor, borrowed $40 to make some technical improvements to a pre-existing sewing appliance. In 1851 Singer received a patent for his invention, the world's first practical sewing machine. While the device totally revolutionized the making of clothes and textiles around the world, Singer's company went even further by reinventing the way that the product was marketed to the public.

It was actually Singer's partner and lawyer, Edward Clark, who devised a plan to contract with independent dealers in various retail locations to sell the new machine. By 1856 Singer and Clark had established relationships with fourteen branch stores, where attractive young women were hired to demonstrate the sewing machines. The price tag on the new contraptions was a whopping $100—at a time when most Americans made only about $500 a year. To help sell the expensive product, Singer and Clark originated two other

Versatile, progressive, and full of opportunity, Quixtar represents the Internet and ecommerce at their best.

Quixtar is the perfect symbol of this new age of innovation, which will reshape our world in the twenty-first century. Like no other company on or off the Internet, Quixtar skillfully weaves together new technologies in a way that greatly improves our lives. But even more important, Quixtar gives each of us the opportunity—no matter what our background, gender, income, or education—to play a leadership role in the Internet Revolution.

commercial innovations that changed the business world: the trade-in allowance (bring in your old, pre-Singer sewing machines and receive a $5 allowance toward a new machine) and the installment-buying plan (take a machine home today and pay only $5 a month until it's all paid for). Both new sales methods revolutionized business. In 1880 the Singer company sold over 500,000 machines.

When they introduced the first electric model in 1889, they started selling over a million machines a year—most of them through independent, contracted sales agents. The Singer company became the world's first multinational corporation and created a brand name that is now known in 150 countries around the globe.

After the turn of the twentieth century, Singer and Clark's novel distribution system began to catch on with the new automobile manufacturers and soft drink companies. Local dealers and bottlers bought licenses to distribute and represent the products in defined territories. Other industries followed suit in the 1920s and 1930s and began to adopt the franchise method: oil and gas companies, drug stores, grocery chains, auto parts stores, and restaurants. By the time milk shake–machine salesman Ray Kroc began selling McDonald's franchises in 1955, franchising had become a proven and appealing method for distributing a wide variety of products and services.

Franchising completely changed the face of business around the world. Here at the dawn of the twenty-first century, franchising now accounts for an amazing $1 trillion in estimated sales in the United States alone. There are over 2,500 franchisers, close to 600,000 franchisees, and nine million people employed by the franchising industry.

Direct Sales

Referral-based marketing owes much to this tradition of franchising but also has its roots in the sales innovations that originated in the Corporate Revolution of the late 1800s. Prior to the birth of big industrial corporations, small companies lacked the financial strength to really invest in sales and advertising. They relied primarily on regional and local merchant networks to sell their wares. Traveling salesmen of the nineteenth century—known at the time as "drummers"—received little or no training, guidance, or support. They were paid on commissions only and hired for one-year terms (contracts were frequently terminated on short notice for low sales). The drummers—who were most often not even assigned specific territories—spent a great deal of their time on the road, zipping back and forth across the country on the new railroads.

But as corporations came on the scene, with large amounts of capital to put behind their sales force, the old learn-as-you-go, sink-or-swim drummer system soon became a thing of the past. As historian Olivier Zunz writes: "The formation of very large sales departments by corporations led to professional salesmen. The new science of salesmanship was distinguished by its recognition of ethical principles as well as its emphasis on carefully planned strategies."

Corporations made sales one of the new white-collar professions of the early 1900s. Large businesses paid their salesmen a regular salary; hosted extravagant sales meetings that included lavish dinners, award ceremonies, and social activities; and created training systems to help guide and motivate new recruits. Salesmen were focused on specific territories and taught to deal directly with customers and clients. Interestingly enough, Thomas J. Watson, who founded IBM in 1924—which would later lead the computer revolution and make the Internet possible—started out as a salesman in 1895 for the National Cash Register Company, one of the companies that championed the new direct-sales movement.

At the heart of the inventive training systems was a totally new philosophy of sales. "Salesmanship," Zunz continues, "was no longer a collection of mere procedures and rehearsed spiels to get the customer's signature on the dotted line. It was a moral crusade that could be undertaken only by principled men. It involved a 'constant endeavor to improve oneself' . . . Salesmanship became the means of realizing one's best inner qualities and inducing customers to realize theirs. Moral and ethical rigor were a prerequisite for financial success."

Like franchising, corporations began making good use of these new sales methods in the late 1800s as proven, effective ways to distribute their products and services to the public. In 1910, reflecting the growth of the industry, the Direct Selling Association was founded. Today the DSA represents over 25 million people worldwide (almost 10 million in the United States) who participate with over 140 companies in a nearly $80-billion-a-year global industry.

THE REFERRAL-BASED marketing business model was the offspring of both franchising and the new sales movement that originated in the Corporate Revolution of the late 1800s. Referral marketing capitalized on what is best about each: namely, the opportunity for achievement, wealth, and independence, backed up by a proven training and support system.

As a business opportunity, Quixtar combines those elements of franchising that make it an alluring and promising option for entrepreneurs, with the benefits of direct sales—

access to superior products, training, motivation, and recognition. By systematically shaping these tried-and-true business practices into one unique model and tying it with emerging Internet technology, Quixtar has taken a quantum leap forward into the twenty-first century.

How It Really Happened

SO FAR, WE'VE learned that referral-based marketing has its roots in the Corporate Revolution, with innovations in franchising and direct sales. But just how were they brought together? The answer is a fascinating story that begins nearly eighty years ago.

A Vita, Huh?

The best place to begin our tale is China in the 1920s. Carl Rehnborg, working as a manufacturer's sales agent during Chiang Kai-shek's revolutionary unification of China, began noticing the effects of diet and nutrition on the health of the people around him—especially during his stint in an internment camp when food was scarce. It was during his years in China, 1915 to 1927, that Rehnborg began to formulate the concept of a nutritional food supplement. When he returned to the United States, Rehnborg settled in an apartment loft on Balboa Island near Newport Beach, California. Over the next few years Rehnborg turned his small home into a research lab as he investigated ways to turn unrefined plant materials into digestible capsules.

Keep in mind that the concept of a vitamin supplement was totally new. In fact the word *vitamin* didn't actually appear until about 1920, as biochemists studied enzymes and digestion. Throughout the 1920s and early 1930s there were breakthroughs made in some of the best research labs in America, Britain, and Germany that furthered the understanding of vitamins and their effects on health. Working on his own in a makeshift lab, with no university or government funding to support him, Rehnborg was as much an inventor as he was a scientist. His guiding concept—decades ahead of its time—revolved around a natural, proactive approach to health and nutrition. Rehnborg's novel idea was that natural, uncooked greens could be somehow concentrated into pill form, which in turn could be added to one's diet to improve health.

Rehnborg launched "California Vitamins," the world's first multivitamin, multimineral food supplement in 1934 (just two years after the discovery of Vitamin C). In 1939 he changed the name of the fledgling company to "Nutrilite Products." Rehnborg sold and gave away samples of his strange new pills to family and friends but had difficulty marketing the product to a larger audience. A "vita" huh? many folks probably wondered. In desperation, Rehnborg even tried paying people to simply recommend the product and talk it up among their friends. Sales improved, but only somewhat.

IN 1945, AFTER years of struggling to find the best way to distribute his innovative product, Rehnborg was joined by the marketing team of Lee Mytinger and Carl Casselberry—a duo that had previously worked with the J. C. Penny Company. Working together, the three combined Rehnborg's commissions-for-referrals approach with a progressive, multilevel compensation plan that would become known as network marketing.

The idea was simple and yet truly revolutionary: Members of the Nutrilite sales force would first use the product themselves, then sell the vitamins to regular customers using a direct sales method. But salespeople also had the freedom to recruit and train their own sales organizations—an empowering approach similar to franchising—for which they would receive commissions as well. Rehnborg handled manufacturing and production, and made sure the vitamins were shipped out on time. Under an exclusive marketing agreement, Mytinger and Casselberry operated the network of independent sales reps, keeping track of volume and the chain of referrals.

With the financial rewards securely in place, the sales force grew exponentially based on a simple word-of-mouth formula. Nutrilite Products—the world's first-ever producer of all-natural vitamins—became quite successful in the postwar boom, with an expanding network of sales distributors around the country.

Hello, Grand Rapids

One of Nutrilite's new sales representatives was Neil Maaskant, a Dutch immigrant who lived in Chicago. Late in the summer of 1949 Maaskant drove up to Grand Rapids, Michigan, to run the Nutrilite opportunity past a relative—a second cousin named Jay Van Andel. Then in his mid-twenties, Van Andel had grown up in Grand Rapids and had spent time in the service during the Second World War. As fate would have it, Maaskant couldn't have picked a better person to introduce to the Nutrilite business.

At the time, Van Andel was sharing a lakeside cottage with his friend-since-high-school, Richard DeVos. Also the descendant of Dutch immigrants, DeVos had grown up in Grand Rapids and was a veteran of the war as well. Both young men were enterprising, to say the least. In the few short years since they had left the service, they had opened, operated, and sold a successful flying school, an air-charter business, and a hamburger stand. By the time Maaskant showed up with his Nutrilite vitamins in August of 1949, the two were seriously looking for a new challenge.

Maaskant talked with DeVos and Van Andel late into the night—discussing the benefits of vitamins and the scope of the Nutrilite opportunity. By the time Maaskant got back in his car to leave, both Rich DeVos and Jay Van Andel had signed on as brand-new Nutrilite distributors. Their only product was a small box of nutritional food supplements—$19.50 for a one-month supply. As for marketing tools, all they had was a small pamphlet—"How to Get Well and Stay Well"—that extolled the virtues of the vitamins.

The American Way

Two weeks later, after only one sale (and that to a friend who was just being nice), DeVos and Van Andel traveled to Chicago to attend a Nutrilite sales meeting. They were both awed by the "big picture" of the vitamin business they had gotten into. They sat and listened intently as Lee Mytinger and successful Nutrilite sales reps addressed the crowd of over one hundred distributors. On the way home that evening, DeVos and Van Andel vowed to make the business work for them.

During the 1950s the duo and a powerhouse team of leaders in their sales force educated people one household at a time about the benefits of proper nutrition and the role of vitamin supplements. They were literally at the forefront of a revolution in preventative health care. Operating as the Ja-Ri Corporation (short for Jay and Rich), they aggressively promoted the products and the opportunity through a network of word-of-mouth referrals. In the process they built one of the most successful Nutrilite distributorships in the country. By the end of the decade, Jay Van Andel was even offered the job of president of Nutrilite—which he turned down to maintain his partnership with DeVos.

FACED WITH INTERNAL challenges at Nutrilite that threatened the viability of the company, DeVos and Van Andel joined a core group of business leaders in their organization in forming the American Way Association on April 30, 1959. Nutrilite had been confronted with serious in-house struggles, and the writing was on the wall. DeVos, Van Andel, and their team of leaders—led by Fred Hansen, Joe Victor, and Jere Dutt—all agreed that they should take steps to make their sales organization more self-reliant and adaptable to the changing business conditions. The founding of the American Way Association was the first step toward making sure that the people who actually did the work would have a direct voice in the policies, procedures, and the decisions of the business.

"That was in 1959, when I was just eleven years old," remembers Jody Victor, a widely acclaimed Quixtar leader, teacher, and entrepreneur. His mother and father, Joe and Helyne Victor, had worked with DeVos and Van Andel in the Nutrilite business since 1951. The Victors were integral players in the founding of the American Way Association.

"I'll never forget it," Jody continues. "It was such an exciting time. We knew something big was happening. Keep in mind that these were full-time Nutrilite salespeople. It wasn't just something they were doing on the side. This is how they earned their living. These people were heroes to me, larger than life. I was in awe of all the hard work they did and the company they were putting together."

The members of the new association, each of whom paid $1 to join, mapped out a plan of action that included the decision to distribute their own exclusive product line. They leaned toward offering common household products that everyone used and that anyone could sell; small ticket items such as soaps and cleaning supplies that had to be replenished on a regular basis. The first item they offered was a biodegradable liquid cleaning compound they called "Frisk."

In retrospect, the FTC case was a testament to Amway's remarkable success. The company had racked up incredible achievements in just over a decade and had fast become a real player in the marketplace. Who *wouldn't* wonder how it had happened? The case against Amway became a test case against the entire referral marketing industry.

"That stuff could clean!" laughs Jody Victor. "It was their first product. We were living in Cuyahoga Falls, Ohio, just outside of Akron. And the place was the rubber capital of the world, with Goodyear, Goodrich, Firestone, General Tire, and some others; all of those factories in one town. When the men in the factories made these tires, they got all this black junk all over them. But Frisk took it off. It was amazing. My father's insurance man actually found the stuff. Somebody was trying to market it for use in homes. The guy that took it to my father said, 'You guys sell those all-natural vitamins. Well, here's an all-natural cleaner. You should sell this, too.' And they did."

Frisk became incredibly successful, as were a number of other early products, including an oven cleaner, a furniture polish, and a concentrated laundry detergent, "SA8." In 1964 all the divisions that had evolved from the American Way Association were officially incorporated as the Amway Corporation. The company was operated out of two office basements in the DeVos and Van Andel households in Ada, Michigan. (By comparison, the Amway World Headquarters complex in Ada today stretches for over a mile and covers almost 400 acres.)

Growth, Growth, Growth

In its first year of business, Amway's estimated retail sales surpassed $500,000—an amazing accomplishment for a brand new company. Word of the superior cleaning products and accessible business opportunities rapidly spread across the United States from friend to friend, family member to family member. Contrary to what is commonly believed, sales in the early years were generated by personal referrals, just as they are today—not by distributors who went door-to-door. In 1960 Amway also held its first annual convention, at the Pantlind Hotel in Grand Rapids. Other notable milestones included:

During the 1960s Amway fine-tuned and clarified the multilevel compensation plan by implementing the Direct Distributor pin levels (such as Emerald and Diamond) to keep track of and reward personal business growth.

In 1962 the corporation became a member of the Direct Selling Association and joined in formulating an industry-wide, uniform code of ethics.

In October, 1962 Amway took referral-based marketing to the world by launching its business opportunity in Canada; that was followed by Australia (1971), the United Kingdom (1973), Hong Kong (1974), Germany (1975), and so on. Today Amway encompasses millions of Independent Business Owners in eighty different countries and territories.

Artistry, the company's enormously successful skin care and cosmetics line, was launched in 1968.

With over 200 items in its product line, the company recorded $100 million in estimated retail sales in 1970.

Coming full circle, Amway acquired a controlling interest in the Nutrilite company in 1972. Today, Amway's Nutrilite division produces one of the most popular brands of vitamin and mineral supplements in the entire world.

Challenge and Victory

The 1970s proved to be a trying time for the Amway Corporation. Despite its runaway success and good fortune, as well as a glowing, nearly forty-year history of referral-based marketing, some began to doubt the integrity of the company's sales plan. In the early '70s the Federal Trade Commission initiated a six-year investigation of the Amway opportunity—putting the corporation and all its distributors under an exacting legal microscope.

Amway had some good company. About the same time that the government was checking them out, FTC attorneys also took on Xerox in another well-publicized case. And during the 1970s, the FTC began regulating the franchising industry as well, laying down new rules that all franchised businesses had to follow.

In retrospect, the FTC case was a testament to Amway's remarkable success. The company had racked up incredible achievements in just over a decade and had fast become a real player in the marketplace. Who *wouldn't* wonder how it had happened? The case against Amway became a test case against the entire referral marketing industry. The court was asked to decide once and for all: Was the Amway plan of marketing products and services through networks of in-home consumers and salespeople a legal way of doing business?

ON MAY 8, 1979, after six years of investigation and four years of legal proceedings, the federal court published its "Final Order and Opinion" regarding the Amway Corporation. While the court dealt with a variety of topics, at the core of the decision was the ruling that Amway's marketing plan was indeed legal and proper. The corporation's celebrated victory thus became the legal precedent and benchmark for other network marketing and direct sales opportunities. Here are a few notable excerpts from the 1979 ruling in the case:

Amway "interjected a vigorous new competitive presence into [a] highly concentrated market by developing what is known as a 'direct selling' distribution network."

"The advantages claimed for a direct selling operation include home delivery, explanation and demonstration of product characteristics and use, explanation of product guarantees, and other similar services. Amway has shown that these advantages can be considerable. One of the reasons for [their] rapid growth is that Amway's products have very high consumer acceptance."

"The Amway Plan does not contain the essential features [of an illegal pyramid], and therefore it is not a scheme which is inherently false, misleading, or deceptive."

Boom Time

Amway continued to enjoy unprecedented growth following the momentous FTC ruling. By 1980 the company's total estimated retail sales surpassed $1 billion—the first company in history to employ referral-based marketing that ever reached such incredible heights.

The Amway Corporation has always had a rich history of joint venturing with manufacturers and service providers. It has excelled in making the products and services of other companies (items in which Amway or its subsidiaries didn't specialize) available to its vast distributor network. If there were ever a company that displayed remarkable expertise in building and maintaining relationships with fellow companies, it is the Amway Corporation. In the wake of the landmark 1979 legal decision, those alliances only multiplied. Corporate America stood in long lines to apply for access to Amway's vast network of Independent Business Owners, a phenomenon that continues to this very day.

The result is that the Amway Corporation has been able to offer its distributors an extremely diverse, top-quality line of products and services that includes everything from Kleenex tissues to Ruffles potato chips to Adidas tennis shoes—not to mention the hundreds of goods that Amway itself produces.

To the folks who hadn't paid attention to what was actually going on, Amway was still some little business that sold soap and shoe polish door-to-door. Whereas actually, the "little" company from Ada, Michigan, was rapidly becoming the world's largest consolidated ordering service, capable of shipping nearly any product or consumable directly to someone's front door—and all of this through a unique word-of-mouth advertising network of consumers.

A WATERSHED EVENT occurred in 1985 when Amway began offering MCI long distance phone service to its distributors—a move that proved to be tremendously rewarding for MCI, as well as a boon to the members of the consumer network. Since the upstart phone company was a publicly traded commodity, brokers on Wall Street perked up as they watched MCI's subscription rate and stock price go through the roof. How did *that* happen? they wondered. The answer: Amway. Amway? The *soap* company? Yes, Amway.

As Wall Street learned a lesson about the power of referral-based marketing, MCI's success fueled the mad dash that corporate America made to Ada, Michigan. Thousands of companies knocked on Amway's door, hoping to introduce their goods into the private network. Ever selective about who they chose to do business with, the corporation's executives diligently considered the merits of each individual company and its products—holding them to an uncompromising, high standard. By the early '90s Amway's product line had grown exponentially, and its immense Personal Shoppers Catalog had become an upscale version of a Sears or J. C. Penny's catalog—complete with an entire gourmet grocery store section. And the word was getting out— fast!—that Amway was doing something no company had ever done before.

"I can't say I completely understand how Amway works," a Fortune 500 executive told me in an interview for this book. "I just know it *does* work, and it works well. Amway's got the formula for success, there's no question about it. They know how to make things happen."

MUCH MORE THAN SOAP

Besides offering hundreds of its own branded products—including everything from cleaning supplies to vitamins to breakfast cereal—the Amway Corporation has a long history of representing major brand name manufacturers and service providers to its vast network of consumers and salespeople. Amway has evolved into a "Canopy Corporation," a central hub through which a wide variety of products and services can be ordered. By the early 1990s, Amway's Personal Shoppers Catalog had become an upscale version of a Sears or J. C. Penny's catalog—plus, it contained an entire gourmet grocery section. Amway's hundreds of merchant partners include:

Adidas	Champion
Anne Klein	Christian Dior
AT&T	Disney
Bell Atlantic	Dockers
Betty Crocker	Duckhead
Broyhill	Frito Lay

General Electric

Goodyear

Hamilton Beach

Hershey's

Hoover

Izod

Kellogg's

Kinko's

Kodak

Magnavox

Minolta

Nabisco

Nikon

Panasonic

Perry Ellis

Playskool

Quaker

Rubbermaid

Sanyo

Singer

Spalding

Sunbeam

Van Heusen

Visa

Whirlpool

Wrangler

Zenith

Success Story

Beginning in the mid to late 1980s, and continuing through the '90s, Amway's growth was nothing short of spectacular. In 1991 estimated retail sales reached $3.1 billion. By 1995 that figure more than doubled to $6.3 billion. In 1997 sales skyrocketed to a stellar $7 billion. Meanwhile, the distributor network was exploding as never before. One notable development during this period was the undeniable professionalization of Amway's ranks. Doctors, lawyers, corporate executives, and high-powered financial experts have come in droves to find out for themselves what the talk is all about.

The story of Amway is one of the great success stories of all time. In less than forty years, a small company from Ada,

Michigan—with one product and a handful of salespeople—
has perfected and fine-tuned referral-based marketing and
built one of the most successful enterprises in the history of
commerce. Their network of Independent Business Owners
encompasses 3 million people in eighty different countries
and territories. In fact, an estimated 70 percent of Amway's
sales are *outside* North America. In 1997 *Forbes* magazine
ranked Amway as twenty-second on its list of the Top 500
Privately Owned Companies. And while we're at it, here's a
few more notable facts from the Success File. Amway is:

- One of the world's largest manufacturers of brand
  name vitamins and mineral supplements.
- Among the world's top manufacturers of cosmetics.
- The fourth-largest U.S. manufacturer of household
  and personal items.
- One of the top corporate contributors to the
  National Easter Seal Society.
- The holder to nearly 300 worldwide patents, with
  hundreds of others currently pending.

Now You Know

In a nutshell, that's pretty much how it all happened. The
Nutrilite company combined franchising techniques with a
direct sales model to sell the world's first vitamins in the 1940s.
The Amway Corporation took that business model—tweaked
it, fine-tuned it, and perfected it—then shared it with people
from all walks of life in countries around the world, offering a
one-of-a-kind business opportunity as well as access to top-
quality products from a variety of brand-name manufacturers.
In the process, the corporation became a massive consolidated

ordering service, creating the world's most expansive network of in-home consumers and salespeople.

Billions Served:
The McDonald's Connection

OWING IN NO small part to the company's astonishing success, most people believe that Amway actually created referral-based marketing. As you now know, that is not true. Even though Amway is the unparalleled giant and leader of the industry, it was not the first. Nutrilite Products preceded Amway, as did a handful of referral-marketing companies—including Fuller Brush, Shaklee, and Avon—that experimented with a similar compensation plan. Following Amway's lead, a host of other companies have successfully employed referral marketing over the last few decades. But the perception persists that Amway was the first.

In the same way, many people believe that the McDonald's Corporation created the self-service restaurant and fast-food franchising. But despite the fact that the trademark golden arches have sprung up around the world, and billions upon billions of hungry customers have been served, McDonald's was not the first to apply the franchise model to the restaurant business. McDonald's story is similar to that of Amway's—both companies took a pre-existing business model and reshaped it to perfection. The triumphs of Amway and McDonald's have much in common. Each built massive companies, made numerous hard-working entrepreneurs extremely wealthy, and became the leaders in their respective industries, thanks to some basic, shared principles. It's important to highlight these principles because they are the very same success factors at the heart of Quixtar.com. Let me show you what I mean.

Firing Up the Grill

In his engaging, behind-the-scenes account of the world's most successful fast food restaurant, *McDonald's: Behind the Arches,* author John Love writes: "Because McDonald's enjoys such a dominant position in fast food, it is understandable why it is widely considered the creator of fast-food franchising and is sometimes perceived as the inventor of all franchising. It was neither." According to Love, the first franchised food establishment was actually an A&W Root Beer stand that opened in 1924. The best-known A&W franchisee was J. Willard Marriott of Washington, D.C., who later converted his root beer stands into the Hot Shoppe's restaurants. He also built a successful hotel business while he was at it.

> **I** can't say I completely understand how Amway works," a Fortune 500 executive told me in an interview for this book. "I just know it *does* work, and it works well. Amway's got the formula for success, there's no question about it. They know how to make things happen."

America's first hamburger chain was Billy Ingram's White Castle, founded in 1921. Another early notable was Bob Wian's drive-in eatery in Glendale, California, called "Bob's Pantry," which started serving up a giant two-patty hamburger in 1937, known as the "Big Boy." And there were also the popular Howard Johnson's restaurants and ice cream parlors, which Johnson began franchising in 1935.

MCDONALD'S GOT ITS start in 1937 when brothers Richard and Maurice McDonald opened a drive-in eatery near Pasadena, California. The twenty-something brothers—sons of a shoe-factory foreman who had lost his job in the Depression—came to California from New Hampshire in 1930 in search of job opportunities. In 1940 Dick and Mac, as the brothers were known, moved to an improved, 600-square-foot space in San Bernardino. In this location, their fast-food formula took off. The brothers invented a speedy, standardized cooking technique and mixed it with elements of self-service to create a new, winning combination.

Within a few years the tiny McDonald's eatery was the talk of the restaurant business, and entrepreneurs from throughout southern California were stopping by to find out the brothers' secret. Dick and Mac happily shared their innovative techniques, which led to a host of copy-cat McDonald's-like eateries—the most famous of which was started by Glen Bell, a telephone repairman and regular McDonald's customer. Bell applied the brothers' success formula to a Mexican menu and founded his own restaurant chain called Taco Bell.

Enter Mr. Kroc

In the summer of 1954 Raymond Albert Kroc (a former professional piano player) paid a visit to the much-talked-about McDonald's hamburger stand. In his McDonald's history, Love writes: "Kroc held the national marketing rights to the five-spindle Multimixers that the brothers used to make their milk shakes, and from his West Coast sales representative, William Jamison, Kroc had been getting a blow-by-blow account of the McDonald brothers' progress for more than a year." To satisfy his own curiosity, Kroc went to see for himself what the McDonalds were all about, and he was extremely impressed.

The McDonald brothers had made previous attempts to franchise their restaurant, but nothing had worked out well. With his background in selling milk-shake machines to a variety of restaurants around the country, Kroc had a valuable perspective on the new fast-food industry. Kroc convinced the brothers that he was the right man to oversee the franchising of their restaurant. In 1955, already in his early fifties, Kroc signed on as McDonald's new franchise agent, vowing to create the nation's first coast-to-coast fast-food chain.

BUT RAY KROC was not alone. By the time he founded his McDonald's System, Inc., on March 2, 1955 (which became the McDonald's Corporation in 1960), a number of other chains had already emerged as competitors: Burger King, Burger Chef, Chicken Delight, and Kentucky Fried Chicken, among others. Convinced that he had the winning formula, Kroc opened his own McDonald's on April 15, 1955, near his home in Des Plaines, Illinois. A showcase of a drive-in (which survives as a museum today), the facility was built as much for customers as it was to interest possible franchisees. After a stop-and-go start, Kroc's plans took hold, and entrepreneurs started lining up to pay the $950 franchise fee to open their own McDonald's drive-ins.

In 1961 Ray Kroc bought the McDonald's business from Dick and Mac for $2.7 million—a tiny fraction of the amount they would have ultimately made had they decided to stay in the fast-food business. In February of the same year, Hamburger University, McDonald's own training facility, welcomed its first class of fifteen students. Located in the basement of a McDonald's in a Chicago suburb, Hamburger University attracted quite a bit of attention, even meriting a spread in *Life* magazine and coverage on the *CBS Evening News*. The restaurant business had never seen anything quite like it.

WITHIN TEN YEARS of becoming Dick and Mac McDonald's new franchise agent, Ray Kroc and his team of store owners made McDonald's not only the most successful fast-food restaurant in the industry but also one of the nation's premiere business opportunities. McDonald's went public for the first time in 1965. According to the company's Web site, a hundred shares of stock costing $2,250 on that day would be worth close to $3 million today. Recognizing its commanding place in American commerce, McDonald's was added to the select thirty-company Dow Jones Industrials Average in 1985. Today, McDonald's thrives as the world's top food-service retailer, with more than 24,500 restaurants in 116 countries. In 1998 McDonald's revenues totaled $18.1 billion—far outdistancing Burger King, which ranked a distant second at $8.2 billion, and Wendy's at $5 billion.

The story of Amway is one of the great success stories of all time. In less than forty years, a small company from Ada, Michigan—with one product and a handful of salespeople—has perfected and fine-tuned referral-based marketing and built one of the most successful enterprises in the history of commerce. Their network of Independent Business Owners encompasses 3 million people in eighty different countries and territories.

Keys to Success

Just what was it that made McDonald's the number one fast-food powerhouse in the world, as opposed to say Burger King, Burger Chef, or Dairy Queen? Under Kroc's leadership, what exactly did McDonald's do differently from all its competitors that vaulted it to the top of the business world?

Likewise, what was it that made Amway one of the most successful privately owned corporations in the history of American business? And what propelled it, as opposed to Shaklee or Avon, to the top of the referral-based marketing industry?

The answers are the same for both companies. McDonald's and Amway have relied on the same keys to success. Below are ten of these principles that, when taken as a whole, are at the heart of both Amway's and McDonald's success. The same principles are now at work on the Internet at Quixtar.com.

1. **The Entrepreneur's Spirit**—The raging fire at the core of both McDonald's and Amway's success is an intense, visionary, entrepreneurial spirit. It was the alluring possibility of achievement, reward, and unlimited opportunity that ignited Ray Kroc when he founded his McDonald's System in 1955. The same passion engulfed Rich DeVos, Jay Van Andel, and their team of business leaders when they founded the American Way Association in 1959. These progressive leaders then imbued their companies' opportunities with that same spirit.

2. **Integrity**—Both Amway and McDonald's rose to the top of their industries by maintaining the integrity and principles that the businesses were founded on.

At the core of both companies is a consistent and unrelenting emphasis on the success of their franchisees and business owners. The success of the whole depends on the success of the individual parts. Neither Ray Kroc nor Rich DeVos and Jay Van Andel have been willing to compromise on that point. McDonald's historian John Love writes: "The essence of Kroc's unique but amazingly simple franchising philosophy was that a franchising company should not live off the sweat of its franchisees, but should succeed by helping its franchisees succeed." The same standard has been at the heart of Amway's marketing plan since day one and is one of the guiding principles behind Quixtar's Independent Business Owner opportunity.

3. **Long-Term Thinking**—It wasn't too long ago that many people considered franchising opportunities—whether restaurants, gas stations, or drug stores—to be nothing but schemes perpetrated by crooked con artists looking to make a fast buck. Some folks even thought of franchising as an illegal pyramid scam. And actually, it was not uncommon to find territory and trademark rights being sold and resold for incredible profits while no stores ever even opened.

Again acting on integrity and an exceptional business acumen, Ray Kroc was committed to an honorable approach. Kroc relied on long-term thinking and a willingness to stay the course, despite the allure of lucrative short-term deals. Unlike some of his competitors, he resisted the urge to sell off huge exclusive territory rights for quick profits. McDonald's was unique in leading the way by selling franchise rights to only one store at a time.

"This is going to be probably one of the most competitive businesses in the U.S.," Kroc told Dick and Mac McDonald in 1958. "And we have the only real solid approach to this business. The other ones are going to die like flies. They are rackets. They are fast-buck deals." Similarly, successful distributors that have affiliated with the Amway Corporation over the years have depended on ethical, long-term thinking to build their businesses.

4. **Synergy**—One of the keystones of both Amway's and McDonald's success has been their ability to build not just one great company but a network of great companies. Love writes: "Ray Kroc's greatest achievement was not at all obvious. He had built not a company but a system of independent companies, all pursuing the same goal, each dependent on the other . . . the synergy that was developing between all the parts of McDonald's was so unique and unexpected. . . . " And: "[McDonald's] is not even a single company. It is a federation of hundreds of independent entities connected by an intricate web of partnerships." The same is true of Amway's global network of business owners, where the whole is actually much greater than the sum of its parts.

5. **Open-Mindedness**—The McDonald's Corporation has always remained open to new ideas, suggestions, and input from its franchisees. For example, the Big Mac and Egg McMuffin sandwiches, and even Ronald McDonald the clown, were all created by individual

store owners in the field, not by advertising reps in a corporate think tank. "The history of the McDonald's System," Love writes, "is the story of an organization that learned how to harness the power of entrepreneurs—not several but hundreds of them." The Amway Corporation has taken the same approach. Like McDonald's, Amway has always treated its independent business owners not as employees or customers but as partners in a common venture.

6. **Willingness to Take Risks**—"The key ingredient in Kroc's management formula," Love writes in *McDonald's: Behind the Arches,* "is a willingness to risk failure and to admit mistakes." Amway and all of its successful business owners would not be where they are today without the very same willingness to learn from their failures and keep striving for success, no matter what temporary setbacks they encountered.

7. **A Training System**—McDonald's well-known Hamburger University has taught thousands of franchisees the tried-and-proven methods of building a successful McDonald's restaurant. That way, there is no mystery to making the franchise work. There is no need to reinvent the wheel. Similarly, Amway's successful business owners have created a proven training system of their own that teaches and supports distributors throughout the network around the world. Without those educational systems, it is doubtful whether Amway or McDonald's would have become the corporate giants they are today.

8. **Anticipating Trends**—Ray Kroc was well aware of the revolution in food service that was taking place

when he began franchising McDonald's. Rich DeVos and Jay Van Andel are alike in that they, too, anticipated and capitalized on change. Time and again, the story is the same: Entrepreneurs and companies that learn best how to anticipate and quickly take advantage of cultural and economic trends will be the success stories of tomorrow. Both Amway and McDonald's are classic examples.

   9. **Conformity with Creativity**—"The fundamental secret to McDonald's success," Love writes, "is the way it achieves uniformity and allegiance to an operating regimen without sacrificing the strengths of American individualism and diversity. McDonald's manages to mix conformity with creativity." Amway, too, expertly manages to mix the creativity of its business owners with commitment to its proven business model. That recipe has created wealth for hundreds of thousands of individuals and families around the world.

   10. **Alliance-Building**—McDonald's blasted to the number-one spot in franchising by building firm alliances with other companies, whether they were suppliers like Coca-Cola or marketing partners like Disney and Wal-Mart. Amway, too, has perfected the art of creating mutually beneficial relationships with corporate America as well as with its networks of business owners—alliances that have ensured the long-term success and viability of the company.

The Quixtar Formula

Both the Amway Corporation and McDonald's used these ten principles to create two of the most successful ventures in the history of commerce. The same standards have been adapted to the emerging Internet technology with the business owners partnering with Quixtar.com. Given the incredible success that this formula brought to Amway and McDonald's, it is a bankable certainty that Quixtar will take its place among the top ecommerce companies in the world. In the next chapter we will take a look at exactly how Quixtar was created by some of the country's most progressive business leaders.

A significant member of the Independent Business Owners Association Board, Brian was an integral player on the team that helped to create Quixtar. A former vice president with the Motorola Corporation, Brian and his wife, Marguerite, enjoy international reputations as two of the most celebrated and acclaimed Quixtar business leaders.

Q. Brian, what's the first thing that comes to your mind when you think about Quixtar?

A. "The timing. The timing couldn't be better. With electronic commerce, we are now witnessing the greatest revolution that has yet occurred in business and marketing. The Internet is becoming the preferred methodology for obtaining goods and services, for shopping, banking, investing, communicating, you name it. And it's just so much bigger than anything that has ever gone before. Whether it's the television or the telephone or whatever, those will all seem pretty meager compared to what's happening with the Internet. With Quixtar, we are perfectly positioned at the forefront of this great new era. The timing could not be better."

Q. I've heard you mention something before that you call the "four cornerstones" supporting Quixtar. Can you explain that?

A. "Sure. I see Quixtar resting strongly on a solid foundation of four cornerstones. The first is the financial backing we enjoy. A lot of Internet businesses will not make it because they are undercapitalized. They may have a great idea, but they're not going to be able to stick it out and make it work because they don't have enough capital. But we benefit from the support of two multi-billionaire founding families that are pulling out all the stops to put this thing together. We go in very, very strong, with two of the wealthiest families in the country supporting us. That's very exciting because we don't have to worry about whether or not Quixtar can be pulled off financially. Every element of the venture will be first class.

"Second, there is the team of architect partners that was brought in to build the Quixtar site. Just think: We're talking about IBM, Microsoft, Fry Multimedia, and others. The very best. They're not going to piece-meal this thing, not at all. They're going with the very top professionals in the high-tech industry to do the best job that's ever been done to date.

"The third cornerstone that supports our success is the variety of major name-brand products and services, all of our online store partners, plus the unique, exclusive items you can't find anywhere else. A lot of companies start with one or two products and then try to build up their offerings as a way to increase spending on their Web sites. But we start with a huge offering of products and services from day one. And then, part of this foundation is that no matter how many products a company has or how good it is, if it doesn't handle the ordering and delivery process well, then it's out of business. That's what people want. They want to click and then have their items show up promptly at the front door in good condition. We've already got eleven service centers strategically located throughout North America. Nobody can beat us in that area. Most of these companies starting up now are scrambling to create the infrastructure that we spent forty years building. We're ahead of the curve, way ahead.

> **W**e are at a unique moment in time, when Quixtar can set the standard for commerce in the new economy. We will be the model for the future.

"The fourth cornerstone is what I call our secret weapon. Not only is Quixtar a high-tech operation, but we bring to the Internet the greatest degree of high-touch marketing that exists in the marketplace today. Through one-on-one, personal, word-of-mouth referrals with friends, neighbors, and relatives, we introduce them to the convenience of shopping online. But even more important, we also show them how they can turn this ordering service into a profit center for their families, if they choose to develop their own Internet businesses. We have an unparalleled incentive to bring people to a Web site where they are tied into the profit loop. This is a tremendous opportunity."

Q. That secret weapon, as you call it, the high-touch aspect of the Quixtar opportunity, is really the key to the whole thing, isn't it?

A. "Yes, I think it is. You know, with everything getting more and more technical today, and machines becoming a greater part of our lives all the time, more than ever people want that one-on-one element, that in-person communication with others. As we begin the twenty-first century, I think the key to success in anything, certainly in business, will be the creation of personal relationships. That has become a priority now more than ever before. Quixtar brings that dimension to ecommerce, far ahead of any other company out there. The Quixtar model of business allows us to work side-by-side with people, not only on the Net but in real life as well."

Q. As a long-standing member of the Independent Business Owners Association and of the Business Operations Committee, you were directly involved in the creation of Quixtar. What was some of the critical thinking that went into your decisions?

A. "We got to a point where we figured out that if our businesses were going to realize their full potential, we needed more than a little fine-tuning or readjusting. We needed a total paradigm shift. We needed a quantum leap that could propel our businesses dramatically ahead into the twenty-first century. The time had come to revolutionize everything we did. With Internet technology powering Quixtar, I think we are perfectly capable of becoming the largest marketing organization in the world. We are at a unique moment in time, when Quixtar can set the standard for commerce in the new economy. We will be the model for the future."

Q. What's the one thing about Quixtar you'd like people to keep in mind?

A. "Most of us have a deep, inner desire to be free and to own our own lives. Quixtar is a tremendous opportunity for people to be able to do just that, without the risk of giving up their current level of income. Quixtar offers a way for people to start their own online companies and tap into the tidal wave of success for the new millennium.

"It's exciting to be able to link up with something that is on the cutting edge of the greatest revolution that's ever happened. And anyone can position himself or herself to take advantage of the rewards that will come about. We are going to witness the greatest wave of wealth that has ever occurred. The Internet Revolution will make the oil, the gold, and the railroad fortunes of the 1800s look very small. In the end, it all comes down to this one question: Why not be a part of making history? Think about it."

One of the most highly respected and regarded Quixtar leaders, Paul Miller is a leader among leaders. Paul served as co-chair on the Growth Committee that actually helped create Quixtar and as president of the Board of the Independent Business Owners Association. Paul and his wife, Debbie, have worked closely with the DeVos and Van Andel families for many years.

Q. Paul, there are a number of reasons why Quixtar.com promises to make Internet history. But if you had to pick just one factor that you think is absolutely critical, what would it be?

A. "Everywhere you look these days, in newspapers and magazines, everyone is talking about the explosive growth of the Internet. It represents the greatest technological and cultural transformation of our time. But I don't think most people feel like they are part of it yet. We hear the news about this or that new billionaire, almost every week. Yet it's always somebody out in Silicon Valley or a twenty-something techie. But what about all the rest of us out here?

"When people turn on the computer and buy from Amazon.com, Jeff Bezos, Amazon's owner, does quite well. But aside from a little convenience achieved by shopping at home, what do you get out of it? Yet now with Quixtar, we're all partners in the venture. This is how all the entrepreneurs out there who don't know how to write computer code can create wealth with the Internet. We're not just saving money and saving time, we're *making* money every time we shop online. We're really a part of it now.

"I think that is the most exciting thing about Quixtar. We're all players now. Instead of sitting up in the bleachers and watching other people become successful with the Internet, all of a sudden we're down on the field making it happen. And the best part of it is that anyone can join us. Anyone who wants to be a leader and benefit from this technological revolution can be a player now."

Q. So, in its essence, Quixtar is all about opportunity?

A. "It's the best thing out there, no contest. And what makes that work is that we have the best business compensation plan on the market today, bar none—especially when you look at the income residuals and bonuses that are available. We've got the sticky factor, built-in, that all the ecommerce sites are trying to get.

"Quixtar gives us points for everything we buy from the site. And those points add up to money. And that money adds up to freedom. It's that simple. Why should I go to a store or shop from another site on the Internet that doesn't affiliate with us? They don't pay me to shop there. Those points will bring my wife home from that job she doesn't like or will send my kids to college or will pay off my car—you see what I mean? Quixtar gives us the opportunity to create real wealth by being a loyal, online shopper.

You can't beat that. Overnight, we became the most loyal, stickiest shopping site on the entire World Wide Web. We're it!"

Q. You've worked closely with members of the DeVos and Van Andel families over the years. What's your take on the leadership they've shown in launching Quixtar?

A. "I think we've really got to applaud the DeVos and Van Andel families for reacting so quickly to the Internet and for taking the initiative as they have. Everyone has been really impressed with their commitment to making sure this was all done right. It would have been so easy for the families to just sit there and say, 'We're doing all right. We've got a multi-billion-dollar empire of companies. Why do we have to care about the Internet? We're doing okay with our businesses all over the world. Why change?'

"But they didn't sit back and just let things happen. They jumped right in there and spared no expense. They offered any resource they had access to so that Quixtar wouldn't be just another shopping site on the Web. That's not their style. They wanted Quixtar to be the new model for business. They wanted it to be the very best."

> I'll tell you this much: the only way you're going to create wealth in a business powered by Quixtar is to be a man or woman of integrity, plain and simple.

Q. One of the things that struck me, in my interviews with Quixtar leaders, is the degree to which money seems to be a secondary reward. There are so many intangibles that success with Quixtar brings—things that you can't really put a price tag on.

A. "That's the part that most people who aren't involved with this business have a hard time understanding. People just aren't used to seeing a business leader go on and on about caring for others and serving other people. That's just not something you hear too much about in the regular business world. When some people first hear it, it makes them wonder if this is even a real business.

"But we're different. That's how our business works. We've got a business model where the more you give, the more you care, the more you work to make other people successful, the more success you will have. Your own success depends on how many other people you can help become successful. That's the element that most people miss. This isn't about rushing out to sign up people to shop on the Internet. This is about developing relationships with people and helping them to see that they can achieve great things in their lives.

"This is not a business where you go off and do your thing and I go off and do my thing, and we sit in our own little cubicles all day long and stare at a machine. Our business model is a web; we're all tied together. We're out there working side by side. We all depend on each other.

"I'll tell you this much: the only way you're going to create wealth in a business powered by Quixtar is to be a man or woman of integrity, plain and simple. We value honesty, we value family, and we value long-term thinking. And we value them not just because it's the right thing to do, but because that's how you become successful with our business model. Yes, there is the potential for incredible wealth with our compensation plan. But success in your own business, fueled by all the advantages that Quixtar offers, will bring you so much more than money."

CHAPTER FIVE

A Star Is Born: The Making of Quixtar.com

URING MY WORK on this book, I got a call from an old friend out in California. The conversation went something like this:

"Coy! What the heck is this Quixtar thing all about?" he blurted out. Evidently, my friend had come across some press coverage about Quixtar, and he was aware that I knew a thing or two about the venture. "This is really amazing," he continued. "This is huge news! I had no idea Quixtar was going to be this big."

"Yeah, it's pretty exciting," I answered.

"Exciting?! I'm blown away," he exclaimed. "Where can I buy some stock? I've never heard of anything quite like this on the Internet. Where did it come from?"

Great question. A lot of people are starting to wonder the same thing. Where exactly *did* Quixtar come from? Almost overnight, Quixtar appeared on the Internet horizon and instantly became one of the biggest and most successful destinations on the Web.

"Well," I began with a laugh, "you can't buy stock."

"You're kidding?" he shot back, disappointed.

"Nope. It's a privately owned company."

"Private?" he asked. "Those people must be geniuses! They've got a gold mine. Quixtar is *privately* owned? I can't believe it."

"Believe it," I confirmed.

"Who is it?—Is it Bill Gates? This sounds like a company Bill Gates would create. Who else would have the money and the influence to put something like this together?"

"Well, Microsoft helped develop the site," I told him, "and IBM was involved, too. But Bill Gates doesn't own it."

"Who is it, then?" he pleaded.

"Have you ever heard of the DeVos and Van Andel families?" I asked him.

"De Van who?" he laughed.

"DeVos and Van Andel. How about the Amway Corporation, ever hear of that?"

"*Amway?* You mean the networking people? Don't they sell cleaning products?"

"Among a few thousand other things, yes," I answered with a laugh. "The same two families that own Amway also created Quixtar. It's another one of their businesses."

"No kidding?" He paused. I could hear him sinking back into his chair. "So no stock, huh?" he asked flatly.

"No stock."

"I'm sure this thing is just going to be one of the biggest sites on the Net," he perked up. "There's got to be some way to make some money on it."

"Well," I said positively, "I'm sure there are some people I could refer you to who could help you with that."

The Pioneers

FOR BUSINESS ANALYSTS, it shouldn't come as a surprise that the DeVos and Van Andel families and their team of business leaders are the primary creative and financial forces behind Quixtar.com. The DeVos and Van Andel families have an impressive history of being at the forefront of new trends. Their array of multibillion-dollar companies have been pioneers in the business world in many ways. Consider just a few:

Referral-Based Marketing—Rich DeVos, Jay Van Andel, and their teams of business leaders led the way in fine-tuning new modes of distribution and sales through networks of individual business owners. No other team of entrepreneurs in the history of the United States has enjoyed so much success from applying referral marketing to business. They have led the industry with an unrivaled buy-back policy and were some of the first to promote a high-standard Code of Ethics for all their distributors.

Business Opportunity—The DeVos and Van Andel families, along with their affiliated business leaders, pioneered one of the world's most accessible and successful business opportunities, partnering the resources of multinational corporations with millions of entrepreneurs here and abroad. One of the principle attractions of the unique marketing plan is a residual income flow that resembles royalties usually earned only by artists and inventors.

Women in Business—The two families led the way in pioneering an entire industry that offers women, in particular, an unprecedented business opportunity: unlimited wealth; no glass ceiling; equal pay and support. Women also earn the choice to be at home with their children, while still being the CEO of their own company.

Earth-Friendly Products—The DeVos and Van Andel families have also led the way in the "green" movement, decades ahead of their time. Long before environmentalism was popular, they oversaw the manufacturing of earth-friendly and biodegradable products on a broad scale. To this day, they are acclaimed for their environmentally-friendly products and recycling efforts.

Concentrated Products—The two families were also pioneers in creating concentrated cleaning agents, like detergents. Now most competing companies have followed suit and routinely advertise their own concentrated formulas.

Emphasis on Health—Beginning when Rich DeVos and Jay Van Andel were involved with Nutrilite—the founding company of the vitamin supplement industry—the two families have owned companies that were leaders in promoting health and nutrition. In 1986, for example, they launched their celebrated "Better Life Institute," which produces healthful prepared foods.

Computer Technology—For decades the DeVos and Van Andel families have been pioneers in integrating computers with business to improve the opportunities available to their affiliates. Their companies now boast some of the nation's top Internet-savvy technology departments in the entire world.

GIVEN THEIR TRACK record, it's no wonder that the DeVos and Van Andel families would be one of the first teams of entrepreneurs to take advantage of emerging

Internet technology—and that they would hit a home run on their first try. That they and their business leaders would have a hand in creating one of the biggest ecommerce sites on the Web is no shocker at all, especially for those of us who have tracked their progress over the years. They are simply doing what they do best: pioneering in the world of commerce, pursuing innovative uses of new technologies, anticipating trends, and creating yet another opportunity for entrepreneurs.

An Idea Whose Time Had Come

THE STORY OF how Quixtar was conceived and brought to life begins in the early 1990s, just as the World Wide Web was revolutionizing the Internet. A series of key events set the stage for the emergence of Quixtar. Even from this short distance in time, we can see how historic these events were.

Where exactly *did* Quixtar come from? Almost overnight, Quixtar appeared on the Internet horizon and instantly became one of the biggest and most successful destinations on the Web.

The Prelude

Beginning in 1990, the most striking development at Amway was the unprecedented growth that caught the attention of the entire corporate world. The corporation's unique marketing strategy had become the business opportunity of choice for a whole new generation. Professionals, especially physicians and attorneys, scrambled to sign up as distributors. Many of them discovered that referral marketing was more profitable and more rewarding than their previous pursuits had been. Generation

X-ers, which surveys reveal to be the most entrepreneurial generation America has ever produced, signed up in record numbers. Amway strengthened its position as one of the premiere business opportunities in the world.

Sales tripled during the '90s to a whopping $7 billion in 1997. With more than 400 of their own products, as well as 6,500-plus name-brand products from other manufacturers, Amway's worldwide distribution network was as unique as it was successful. The '90s also saw the corporation expand its opportunity into an additional twenty-nine international markets—including Mexico (1990), Brazil (1991), Poland (1992), Turkey (1994), China (1995), and even India (1998). Throughout the Amway world there was a sense that it was indeed the beginning of a new era for the company.

AT HOME IN Ada, Michigan, there were significant events that made this new era even more apparent. In a move that they had discussed and planned for years, Rich DeVos and Jay Van Andel passed the baton of leadership to their children. In 1993 DeVos's eldest son, Dick, became president of the corporation. Steve Van Andel succeeded his father as chairman two years later, in 1995. Additional members of the second generation of Amway's two founding families have since assumed priority positions within the company as well.

Other changes followed. By 1996 the corporation had instituted its "Direct Fulfillment Program," which allowed any distributor (not just "directs") to order by phone and receive direct delivery of products—including food, clothing, electronic equipment, and, yes, even laundry detergent. With a network of warehouses around the world, its fleet of trucks and planes, plus a talented pool of 14,000 employees, the DeVos and Van Andel families had created the world's foremost order-consolidation service, capable of directly shipping nearly any product to two-thirds of the world's population.

Then, in September of 1997, the company implemented an "Automatic Replenishment Program," which allowed distributors to design their own standing orders and have them automatically home-delivered at regular intervals. That way, your peanut butter and jelly, for example, would show up on your doorstep once every week like clockwork, without your ever going to the store or picking up the phone to place an order. By the middle of 1997, under the leadership of the second generation of DeVoses and Van Andels, many facets of the business were being refined and improved. It was in this environment of change that some of the company's top business leaders put their heads together to map out a plan of action for the twenty-first century.

New Ideas

In 1997 a select committee of business leaders was appointed to develop new ideas about growing their traditional opportunity into the next century. This "growth" committee was the brainchild of living legends Dexter Yager and Bill Britt, two of the most successful entrepreneurs in the history of American business. Both Britt and Yager had agreed that emerging technologies represented possible advantages that were definitely worth pursuing, and that the Internet was unquestionably a factor to be reckoned with.

A former corporate executive, Jim Floor and his wife, Margee, are two of the most successful and renowned Quixtar leaders. As a member of the Independent Business Owners

Association and as chair of the Business Operations Committee, Jim was one of the key players who got the Quixtar ball rolling.

"It really started in 1997," Jim recalls. "I was fortunate to have served on the Growth Committee, which was a team of eight experienced business leaders who came together from various parts of the country and Canada to brainstorm new ideas for taking our businesses into the twenty-first century."

Jim remembers that the Growth Committee didn't necessarily start out with a whole new business plan in mind. "We looked at a bunch of different things," he says. "They were strictly brainstorming meetings—just throw anything out on the table; no judgments. It became apparent after a relatively short period of time that what we wanted to do was totally modernize the business—streamline things. It also became clear that the best course of action was to take our business model and somehow tie it in with electronic commerce. We had all been paying close attention to what was happening with the Internet, and we knew ecommerce was here to stay. So we talked about different approaches we might take along those lines."

ANOTHER KEY MEMBER of the Growth Committee was Tim Foley, a former professional football player and broadcast sports announcer. With a team of business owners that spans the globe, he and his wife, Connie, are two of the most respected, well-known, and accomplished Quixtar leaders.

"I remember we had notes up all over the walls," he says with a chuckle. "We just kept coming up with ideas. Get an idea, write it down. Get another idea, write that down, too.

The whole purpose was to take a fresh look at what we were doing, start with a clean slate, and to think completely outside of the box—practice thinking bigger. We kept asking ourselves: What can we do to make things better? In an ideal world, if we could do anything we wanted to, what changes would we make? That's what it was all about—improving things and coming up with new ideas."

The Technology Development Group

The Growth Committee benefited from periodic research reports of the Technology Development Group (TDG), an advisory panel of scientists and high-tech experts (all of whom were affiliated business owners) who made it their business to stay current on the latest developments in new technology. Brad Doyle, now a member of the Independent Business Owners Association Board and a successful Quixtar leader, was involved in the founding of the TDG.

"The TDG actually started meeting on a monthly basis in March of 1995," Brad said. "We first advised the DeVos and Van Andel families, and then later the Business Operations and Growth Committees, and the Board, about what was going on with the World Wide Web. We also looked at CD-ROM technology, interactive television, digital satellites, you name it. The idea behind the TDG was this: We wanted to explore ways that we could use the new communications technologies to reduce the cost of business while increasing productivity and profitability. That's what we were after. After some research, it became abundantly clear that the Internet would be the technology of choice for the new economy. We knew that would be the way to go."

Best of Both Worlds

The initial ideas that emerged from the meetings of the Growth Committee in 1997 and 1998 essentially had to do with taking Amway to the Internet—using the Web as a new form of distribution for the pre-existing business: progressive thinking, to be sure, but not exactly revolutionary. The more the members of the committee discussed the merits of the concept, however, the more they realized that wasn't the right way to go.

After a series of meetings among themselves and with the DeVos and Van Andel families and their top management team, something totally new began to emerge, something truly revolutionary.

"When you look at the Internet," Jim Floor explains, "there are two basic models of business that can be introduced there. One is an existing company that wants to have a Web presence. The other is a company that does not have an existence at all today, has no history, but says, 'We're going to build from scratch right on the Net.' There are advantages and disadvantages to both models. Some of the advantages of having an existing business are that you already have a client base, you've got a facilitation team in place, and you've got a proven track record and the finances to back you up. The downside of the model is that you also carry a lot of baggage with you. You might even have a management team that is not necessarily knowledgeable or sophisticated about Web business. And you also very often get into conflict with yourself by competing with your own brick-and-mortar stores. One of the problems with Barnes and Noble, for example, is that as they've tried to compete against Amazon, they have found that not all their normal retail outlets are excited about marketing books on the Internet. And why would they be? Now people don't have to go in their stores anymore.

"Those are the two models we looked at," Jim continues, "And I've got to give credit to the corporation on this. The management team and the founding families began to see clearly that we were perfectly positioned to take advantage of *both* models—we could have the best of both worlds. By forming a whole new business model and a whole new company to launch that business model, we could launch a new concept designed specifically for the Internet. It hadn't been done yet. It would be the first of its kind. They developed the idea of a totally new, totally unique business model, which had evolved out of all our brainstorming on the Growth Committee. And, of course, once we understood what they had in mind, we embraced that idea and have worked closely with them over the last year to make that a reality."

Way Beyond

The concept of a completely new, Web-based business model designed specifically for the Internet was first presented to the members of the Growth Committee on Monday, October 12, 1998, in a conference room at the Grand Plaza Hotel in Grand Rapids, Michigan. Attending that momentous meeting were all eight members of the committee, each of them powerhouse business leaders with global organizations, as well as representatives of the DeVos and Van Andel families who were overseeing the project.

The initial reaction? "To a person, we were excited about it," Jim Floor says. "It just made sense. It made a whole lot of sense."

The "ecommerce venture" was still just an idea with no name and little in the way of specifics when it was next presented to the entire thirty-member Board of Independent Business Owners on Thursday, October 15. The IBO board represents the three-million-strong global network.

The critical component of the idea then taking shape in late autumn of '98 was that it went *beyond* taking the traditional Amway business to the Internet—way beyond. The venture would rely on the experience of the DeVos and Van Andel families and on the infrastructure of their many companies, and apply what had always worked best about the opportunity. But it would be something altogether different, *a new company*—and not just a new company but a completely novel way of actually doing business. It would be something Amway could never be, and would be capable of things the traditional Amway business model could never do.

But it would be something altogether different, *a new company*—and not just a new company but a completely novel way of actually doing business. It would be something Amway could never be, and would be capable of things the traditional Amway business model could never do.

And even more important, referral marketing would only be part of the formula. Most of the conventional concepts of network marketing would simply not apply anymore. The Internet venture would branch out to include "member benefits" for those individuals who liked the convenience of shopping at the site but preferred not to get involved as a business owner. It would offer an accessible "client" option, opening the door to the product line in an unprecedented way. And it would integrate new technologies into the design that would profoundly revolutionize the idea of a home-based business. Perhaps unwittingly, the planners of the project had sailed into uncharted waters. In their pursuit to streamline and improve an old business model, they instead created an original archetype for the twenty-first century.

As an Internet-based, ecommerce business, the concept would certainly be high-tech and would capitalize on rapidly emerging technologies. But as a *people* business, with face-to-face interaction at the heart of the process, the concept would offer a high-touch aspect that ecommerce companies have so far failed to provide. To say that it would simply be Amway on the Internet would be like describing an automobile as nothing more than a horseless carriage.

"At the time," Jim says, "there weren't a lot of specifics to go on. It was all just starting to come together. But the key element was that it would be a *new* business model specifically created for Internet technology, as opposed to taking the old business model onto the Internet. And the distinction is significant when you begin to understand the ramifications of each. We all left the meeting that weekend really excited about it."

The Buzz

Word of an ecommerce project filtered out among the business leaders immediately after the historic meeting in Grand Rapids. By the following Monday morning, the buzz had started to spread.

"I first heard about it at a 'Q-12' leadership conference in early November of '98," says Bert Gulick, a celebrated

Quixtar leader and teacher. Together, Bert and his wife, Terri, have built a global business of Independent Business Owners. "We had already heard some rumors going around for about four or five days, something about the Internet and ecommerce. So, yes, we were prepared for some big news. At the conference we went to, there was a representative from the corporation's tech department who presented what he knew about the project. Actually, he didn't know that much himself since he'd just heard about it a few days before. He told us a totally new Internet company would be launched on September 1, 1999. It was going to be a real challenge, he said, to get everything ready by then. But the DeVos and Van Andel families had decided that they were going to do whatever they needed to do to make it happen on that time schedule. We knew right away that this was going to be one of the biggest things to hit the Internet. I even videotaped the presentation that morning because I knew that it was history in the making."

Over the next few days and weeks, talk of the new cyber-company spread like wildfire through networks of business owners around the world. Reports, updates, and rumors of the venture were passed back and forth through voicemail, via e-mail, and at business meetings. As one direct distributor later remarked: "It was electrifying. It's all we talked about, even though nobody really knew much. We all kept asking each other the same questions: How would it work, and what would it be called? But nobody had any answers yet. There were a lot of rumors there for awhile—a lot of rumors and a whole lot of excitement."

Who You Gonna Call?

Meanwhile, back in Ada, the DeVos and Van Andel families and their management team had set about developing a plan of action to make the proposed venture a reality. With the green light of support from the business leaders, it was time to get down to work. The goal was to launch the new Internet-based company on Wednesday, September 1, 1999, which at that point was only ten months away—not a lot of time, to say the least.

It was a daunting task—creating and launching the world's ideal ecommerce site in just under ten months. Without hesitation, the DeVos and Van Andel families pledged whatever resources might be needed, financial and otherwise, including a capable Information Technology (IT) group of nearly 100 talented computer wizards. But that team had never created a commercial site this big, this intricate, and under this kind of deadline.

They needed expert advice from a crew who had actually done something similar to what they were trying to do—who could give them the advice, the support, and the knowledge that it would take. But who? Who would *you* call?

Enter Microsoft

Who else? Founded in 1975 when personal computers were just emerging onto the scene, Bill Gates's multibillion-dollar Microsoft Corporation has become the global leader in the computer software industry. Thirty-five-year-old Stephen McCarty is a managing consultant with Microsoft's Consulting Services (MCS). Formed in 1990, MCS provides technical support and solutions to a variety of business customers, covering a wide spectrum of ventures. MCS has proved to be one of the nation's best consulting firms when it comes to helping businesses make the transition to the new Internet economy.

"The call came in around late October or early November of '98," McCarty remembers. "We were told that the DeVos and Van Andel families were looking at developing an ecommerce site, and they asked if Microsoft would come up to Ada and show them what we could offer in the way of support. We had several different meetings, many different whiteboard and PowerPoint presentation-type sessions. We weren't the only consulting service being considered at the time. But in the end, we were awarded the opportunity to work on the project."

During a pre-launch interview in the summer of 1999, McCarty said the creation of Quixtar was a watershed event in the history of the Internet. "We're really excited about this," he told me. "We're not only anticipating great success with Quixtar, but it also opens up a whole new realm of opportunities in ecommerce. It's the beginning of a new era. From day one you're going to see tremendous growth with Quixtar, I'm sure of it."

McCarty confirmed that throughout the development process, there has been a great deal of interest and excitement about the project. "I've received calls from all over the world, as far away as Asia, from people who just want information about Quixtar. The project has also generated a lot of interest in ecommerce from other companies—people who previously hadn't expressed any interest in the Internet. It's clear that ecommerce is becoming a way of life, and Quixtar has made a lot of people sit up and take notice."

A New Paradigm

Now that Microsoft was in place as the key development consultant on the project, the planners next turned to the process of selecting a solutions partner to actually help write the computer code that would bring the ideal ecommerce site to life.

"When we got started," McCarty recalled, "our first step was to internally evaluate our Certified Solutions Providers, the development companies we partner with. We wanted to make sure that we put the right partner on this project, one that understood the complexity of ecommerce and that had already had some success in that area. We narrowed it down to three or four finalists that fit that description. I think it was around late December of '98 that we picked Fry Multimedia. So starting in early January we were off and running. And there was a lot we had to do."

Founded in 1993, Fry Multimedia has had a hand in creating some of the best-known, most successful ecommerce sites on the Internet—including 1-800 Flowers, Eddie Bauer, Godiva Chocolatier, MSN Shopping, and Staples. Fry's position in the venture would be to develop the necessary ecommerce architecture to support the Quixtar site. In January 1999 representatives from Fry and Microsoft joined the 100-strong IT team for weekly meetings in Ada.

The first priority was laying down a series of monthly goals and milestones to ensure that everything was ready for the launch in September. As Microsoft coordinated the communication between all the parties and offered training sessions for the IT group, Fry Multimedia's tech team started outlining the site's parameters. The launch of the new company was then less than eight months away.

Bridget Fahrland is Fry Multimedia's associate director of interactive marketing. "We were all aware from the beginning that Quixtar was going to be much more than your average ecommerce site," Fahrland said during a pre-launch interview. "It was something new. There is a dimension to it that other ecommerce sites just don't have. Quixtar comes to the Internet with an established customer base, and a lot of implications that the average ecommerce site doesn't have. Quixtar is a brand-new paradigm for ecommerce."

Tridigital Commerce

John Parker is the Director of Business Relations for Quixtar. He has been closely involved with the project since the very beginning. In a conversation just days before the launch of Quixtar.com, John and I talked about some of the opportunities that the Internet had brought to marketing.

"In the early stages of the process," he told me, "we knew that to just refine our old business model and stick it on the Web wouldn't work. We knew that wouldn't work because we had watched other industries and companies try to do just that. We quickly came to the conclusion that technology alone isn't what's going to make you succeed on the Web. We saw clearly that the companies that were going to succeed long-term on the Web, that were going to lead the way in the new economy, would be the companies that created all new business models and integrated them with the new technology. The conventional approaches just wouldn't work in this new medium.

"The common thread that we saw running across all the ecommerce sites on the Web," he continued, "is that they were still relying on the old business model. The old model says that you run advertising to drive people somewhere, and you sell them goods and services once they get there. The problem with that, when you factor in the way this technology works, is that the cost of customer acquisition is so high that companies are struggling to find ways to make that old formula profitable. And the vast majority of them just can't do it. We do not think that traditional business model will work on the Web. You have to find other ways to link up with customers.

"As we look across the whole gamut of what other industries are doing, we aren't that interested in exactly who's going online. What interests us is who's reinventing their business by using the new Internet technology in a different way. Plugging into the Web isn't enough anymore. You've got to be willing to totally innovate; not just improve what you had been doing, but reinvent it in every way possible.

"As Quixtar evolved, we started to watch this new business model emerge. We developed *tridigital commerce* as the catch-phrase to describe what Quixtar.com was all about. Tridigital commerce encapsulates the leveraging of new technology into a business model that creates an incredible opportunity for Web-based entrepreneurs, with a unique shopping experience that the Internet has not yet seen. It's the first of its kind."

I asked John Parker what had been the most challenging aspect of the venture.

"Part of what was difficult about this was that we had no examples to look at," he answered. "There were no models to compare ourselves to. No one else had done anything like this. When we started out, we couldn't look at anything that had already been done to get an idea what we wanted to do.

We were told by the experts that nothing like this had ever been done on the Internet. Quixtar represents a completely original business model."

Countdown 9-1-99

In late January 1999, the IT group posted a promotional site for the new ecommerce venture on the Internet. The pilot site—*Countdown 9-1-99*—boldly announced: "Starting a web-based business can require an army of computer wizards and cost millions of dollars. But, beginning September 1, 1999, you can start your own ecommerce business with the computer knowledge you already use at home or work."

Available on the site were the latest ecommerce statistics documenting the exploding Internet economy, the growth of online shopping, as well as an outline of some opportunities that would be offered by the upcoming, still-to-be-named business. The countdown site gave interested Net surfers a chance to register for information about the opportunity as it became available. In just a few short weeks, nearly a quarter of a million people had signed up for the updates. As the excitement mounted, the countdown site tallied over *1 million hits a day.* One week it received over *9 million hits,* an extraordinary amount by any standard, especially considering that the promotional site offered nothing for sale and had only about ten pages of content.

Pushing the Envelope

Finally, in early March, after months of speculation and rumors, representatives of the DeVos and Van Andel families released an official announcement about their Internet venture, including the long-awaited name of the project. The press release hit the news wires at exactly 6:59 A.M. Eastern Standard Time on Wednesday, March 3, 1999.

Dateline: Ada, Michigan: "The launch of Quixtar (pronounced QUICK-STAR), a new business model developed specifically for the Internet, was announced today by the DeVos and Van Andel families, who will support this new venture in the U.S. and Canada with their considerable global resources. The new ecommerce site, which will launch September 1, will provide a unique web-based business opportunity for entrepreneurs and offer high-quality products and services to Internet shoppers. A Quixtar business will reward entrepreneurs for delivering new customers and members to www.Quixtar.com through bonuses earned on the sales volume they generate."

The two-page release also included a quote from Ken McDonald, now the senior vice president and managing director for Quixtar: "The DeVos and Van Andel families developed a direct selling giant that was ahead of its time and on the cutting edge of marketing. With Quixtar, we're pushing the envelope once again."

"This is a new business using new technology for the new millennium," David Van Andel was quoted as saying. "We believe this is the future for business and we need to be in front of the curve so that we and the independent business owners we support will benefit from this growing trend."

Reports of Quixtar rapidly surfaced in newspapers and magazines, as well as in a variety of publications on the Net. The offices of business leaders across the country were flooded with press calls for more information and sound bytes. From Los Angeles to Washington, Detroit to Miami, word of Quixtar was front-page news. However, most writers were unfamiliar with the specifics of the project and incorrectly assumed that Quixtar was simply going to be an Internet version of the traditional Amway business. Few reporters grasped the significance of Quixtar as a totally unique and separate venture.

It was a critical point that many reporters missed: As a stand-alone ecommerce company, Quixtar was neither a part nor a subsidiary of the Amway Corporation. And the Independent Business Owners who affiliated with Quixtar would not be *in* Amway any more than they would be *in* Microsoft or *in* IBM. Quixtar would benefit from the Amway Corporation's infrastructure—its vast warehouse space, phenomenal customer service, and unmatched consolidated ordering services—and take advantage of its incredible compensation plan. But beyond that, Quixtar was out there on its own, blazing a brand new trail in a brand new marketplace.

Still Climbing

While business leaders and corporate executives fielded a barrage of questions, a handful of tech experts worked around the clock on-site in Ada, Michigan, to meet their monthly goals. Representatives from IBM made sure all the hardware and servers were in place. Web site builders from t-dah!, a division of C-E Communications—another Michigan-based multimedia firm—oversaw the look and feel of Quixtar. And they were joined by talent from the Vignette Corporation, who developed the site's information management and personalization capabilities.

"There's never been anything done like this," Quixtar leader Brad Doyle told me during an interview. "This is absolutely the biggest, most impressive site that has ever hit the Internet. We're talking up to 20,000 pages of content, and it's still climbing."

A technical expert who has worked with personal computers since they were first invented, Brad quickly sketched out the intricacies of Quixtar's high tech aspects.

"They've got 150 programmers working full time," he explained, "multiple DS3 circuits; triple redundancy built into the system; plus multiple server farms, and 128-bit encryption."

And it's the eminently high level of encryption that will ensure that all credit card transactions are perfectly safe.

"The safest thing you can do with a credit card is to put it on a computer server that's encrypted at 128 bits," Brad said convincingly. "Whether you give your credit card to a restaurant, a gas station, or a hotel, those are all more dangerous than entering the number on a secured Web site, especially one encrypted with 128 bits. Besides, there are no cases of credit card fraud on a secured Web site to date. When it's all said and done, I believe this will be one of the great early myths of the Internet: that entering your credit card number on a secured Web site is some kind of a risk. It's not at all."

Scope Creep

In July, Microsoft began subjecting the site to a battery of stress-tests to gauge how many hits it could take. "We just want to double-check the infrastructure," Stephen McCarty said. "We have been told that it needed to be able to support a tremendous number of hits on a daily basis. So we're going to keep testing it and make sure it can withstand the load. We're expecting this site to be extremely busy."

I asked McCarty what had been the biggest challenge so far in creating Quixtar. "When you have this large of a project," he answered candidly, "there's always room for what we call *scope creep,* where a project tends to get off track. What happens is, in most large-scale projects, you have users who think something up and then they will immediately want to add it to this current project. And what ends up happening is it detours the project, throws the project behind schedule. Scope creep is probably one of the biggest causes for projects not to be delivered on time. Quixtar is so big and unique, it's natural to except some scope creep here and there. So we've had to keep an eye out for that. But overall, it really hasn't been that much of a problem. We've hit our monthly goals, and everything is on schedule."

Was it tough building a site this massive in such a short amount of time? "On a lot of projects this size it usually takes a while for decisions to be made," McCarty responded, "but not on Quixtar. Decisions have been made and implemented very quickly. We typically don't see projects move this fast. It's been really impressive, and we've been honored to have been a part of it."

Opening the Door

In early August 1999 the site was opened for beta testing. Approximately six hundred of the Quixtar business leaders were given password-protected access to the site and invited to get the first look at what had been created so far. On Friday, August 6, I was fortunate to have been invited to the home of Quixtar leaders Bo and Sandy Short when they first sat at their computer, dialed into the Internet, and linked to Quixtar.com.

"Wow!" Sandy exclaimed as the first page, sprinkled with vivid graphics, started to download. "This is impressive." Bo leaned forward silently in his chair, eyes on the screen.

"This is the future," he said with a grin. "There it is, right in front of you. The Internet, ecommerce, and the whole world of business will never be the same again."

As they explored the site, clicking to different destinations within the spacious digital realm, the Shorts shared some of their thoughts about Quixtar, then just less than four weeks from its September 1 launch date.

"We just consider ourselves incredibly fortunate to be a part of this," Sandy said, as she navigated the mouse on its pad. "We're humbled by it all. So many people put in long hours to make this thing a reality. And here it is. What you're looking at now will become a part of the lives of millions of people. It's really exciting."

"Right now I can't help but think of the individuals who came together to create Quixtar," Bo said. "They had the vision and the perseverance and the courage to make this dream come true. It's an incredible victory."

Just for fun, Sandy placed a small order before they signed off—children's vitamins for their daughter Taylor, a bottle of shampoo, and some makeup. We all cheered as she clicked the final button and made the purchase official.

LITTLE DID WE know at the time, that click would become a part of Quixtar history. Bo and Sandy Short received the following fax a few hours later, dated August 6, 1:43 P.M.:

"On behalf of the Quixtar development team, I would like to congratulate you on being the very FIRST Independent Business Owners to place a live order via Quixtar.com! The opening of the Quixtar beta test today is truly an historic occasion, and you are now a part of history as the IBOs who placed the first live order via the Quixtar Web site. Thank you for participating in our early testing, and congratulations on being a part of Quixtar history! Sincerely, Randy Bancino, Senior Manager, Internet Business Group, Quixtar."

Into the Future

In less than one year a team of tech wizards orchestrated one of the most magnificent accomplishments ever achieved in the new Digital Age. September 1, 1999, the day that Quixtar opened its virtual doors to the world, will go down as one of the most significant dates in Web history. Quixtar not only embodies the latest in high technology and brings under one roof the best elements of a variety of ecommerce ventures, but it goes further by offering a one-of-a-kind, high-touch aspect greatly missing in the new Net-based economy. Quixtar literally brings people together—and not in some cyber chat room, but face-to-face in real life. It provides a base upon which millions of people will build positive relationships that will enrich their lives.

In creating Quixtar.com, the DeVos and Van Andel families demonstrated their keen ability to anticipate trends, to innovate, and to build synergistic alliances. Also critical to the process from the beginning was the creativity of the numerous established business leaders they have long affiliated with. Their experience and insight was invaluable. Far from stifling or devaluing their input, the founding families recognized that the long-term success of any new venture must begin and end with their loyal network of business owners and customers.

In just a few short weeks, nearly a quarter of a million people had signed up for the updates. As the excitement mounted, the countdown site tallied over *1 million hits a day.* One week it received over *9 million hits,* an extraordinary amount by any standard, especially considering that the promotional site offered nothing for sale and had only about ten pages of content.

Bert Gulick underscored this point when I spoke with him a few weeks before Quixtar's opening day. "The DeVos and Van Andel families," he said emphatically, "could have started Quixtar just like they went out and bought the Orlando Magic basketball team or any number of other companies. They didn't have to share this new venture with those of us in the existing field of distributors. They've got enough money in the bank, the contracts with manufacturers, the energy, and the reputation in corporate America, where they could have easily gone out and gotten it off the ground without us. The second generation of the founding families has shown us that the integrity and trust that was there for forty years is still alive and well."

The story of Quixtar also demonstrates another crucial point: The extent to which the project *evolved* as a concept should not be underestimated. "When we first got started," Jim Floor explained, "we had something like an Internet Mall in mind. But over time, Quixtar became much more than that. Shopping is just a part of it now. It's become a totally unique digital destination. If you look at all the other popular ecommerce sites on the Internet, you can see that they're all aspiring to be like Quixtar. We've become the model."

Given the fast-changing nature of the Internet, we can expect Quixtar to continue its evolution, to adapt, change, and improve during the twenty-first century. The progressive, versatile qualities that support it will be ongoing and will contribute toward making it not only one of the most successful opportunities of the new Internet economy but also an original model that other companies will seek to emulate. Microsoft's Stephen McCarty was right on the mark. Quixtar.com is the beginning of a new era.

QUIXTAR.COM
AS INNOVATION

Remember "Ten Lessons from History for Understanding the Internet Revolution" from Chapter 1? Let's revisit those lessons to appreciate how Quixtar.com stacks up to the great lessons of the past. As you'll see, Quixtar more than deserves to take its place in history as one of the great examples of innovation.

1. **Change Happens**—Human society was forever altered when men and women began domesticating wild animals and farming thousands of years ago. Western society was changed yet again when scholars explored the Muslim library in Toledo, Spain. And society changed even more drastically during the Industrial Revolution. Now Quixtar, an unprecedented business model, heralds a new era. It represents the next great step forward in the Internet economy.

2. **You Matter. Yes, You!**—At the core of Quixtar's success are individuals who pay close attention to the changes going on around them and who have seized leadership positions in the Digital Age. Whether they be from clients, members, or Independent Business Owners, the achievements of Quixtar represent the collected accomplishments of millions of individuals.

3. **Technology Gets Around**—Like the wheel, the printing press, the steam engine, or the typewriter, new technologies gradually become a part of human societies all across

the planet. As we watch Internet technology rapidly expand over the next few decades, we will see more and more people coming online and taking part in the new electronic marketplace. Quixtar will be there to offer them a host of opportunities to improve their lives. Today Quixtar only covers North America, but where the Internet goes, Quixtar will soon follow. It is, after all, a *worldwide* web.

4. **The Secret Is in the Network**—Quixtar illustrates this critical lesson from the history of innovation, not once but three times. Quixtar is a *Triple Network:* the union of networks of businesses and business owners, with networks of machines and computers, with networks of members and consumers. The unique power of Quixtar derives from its position as the central hub connecting this Triple Network.

5. **Commerce Is the Key**—History shows us that innovations in commerce are a critical factor in understanding change. New trade routes sparked the creation of the wheel and of writing. Commercial activity was at the heart of Europe's pre-Industrial Age, the Renaissance, and both the Industrial and Corporate Revolutions. Quixtar.com is the commercial innovation of the Internet that will have a profound and positive impact on millions of lives.

6. **The Revolution Is Pervasive**—As the Internet Revolution continues to unfold, Quixtar and its network of Independent Business Owners, members, and clients will be at the vanguard of the movements that reshape our society during the twenty-first century.

7. **It's Not About the Machine**—At its very core, Quixtar.com is not about the wonders of the Internet, computers, or even convenient online shopping. It is about people, their

families, their hopes, and their dreams for the future. Simply put, the advantages offered by Quixtar.com—convenience, value, quality products, relationships, and knowledge—have to do with improving and enriching lives.

8. **Technology Begets Technology**—You can be assured that the technological design team that created Quixtar is at work right now improving and upgrading the site. Since Quixtar—as Web site, business platform, and network hub—is an emerging technology all its own, we will see it lead to even more impressive versions of itself over the decades to come.

9. **New-Found Wealth Is Part of the Package**—In times of great change, when emerging technologies are combined with new ways of doing business, people get wealthy. You remember the example of the Medicis and their banks during the Renaissance, plus the great corporate leaders in America during the late 1800s. Quixtar represents this lesson from history more than any other ecommerce site on the Internet. As individual men and women take advantage of the opportunities Quixtar offers, unbelievable fortunes will be made. Take note: Some people reading this book at this very moment will one day set their families free by creating residual income flow from businesses powered by Quixtar.

10. **The Secret Formula**—Quixtar is a new business model that was created specifically for the Internet. It is not, as most other ecommerce sites are today, simply the Internet version of a retail store or an interactive mail-order catalog. Quixtar is truly a unique experience. As such, it embodies this all-important lesson from the history of innovation—that new

modes of commerce combined with emerging technologies are signposts of great ages of innovation. Just like the Industrial and Corporate Revolutions before it, Quixtar.com represents the commercial application of new technologies as well as a change in the methods of distribution of goods and services. Quixtar stands poised at the threshold of the New World of the Internet. Let the future begin.

QUIXTAR FAQ
FREQUENTLY ASKED QUESTIONS ABOUT QUIXTAR.COM

Now that you've read about the history that led up to Quixtar and all that went into creating it, let's take a moment to answer a few Frequently Asked Questions about Quixtar.com.

What exactly is Quixtar.com?

Quixtar.com is a site (a place you can go) on the World Wide Web (http://www.quixtar.com). Quixtar.com launched on September 1, 1999. Quixtar is a unique, digital destination that combines numerous Internet services into one. It includes all the perks of an online community—the interactivity and personalization—as well as access to a massive order consolidation service.

What is an order consolidation service?

An order consolidation service (OCS) is a convenience that you can use to access thousands of different products directly over the Internet. It allows you to shop from home for things that you would normally have to go to a store and buy. An OCS is a tool that consolidates all your orders into one online experience by bringing together a variety of options, services, companies, and products in one central location on the Internet.

So I can go shopping at Quixtar online and not have to go to the store if I don't want to?

Exactly. Quixtar brings all the stores to you—at one location, right there at your fingertips in your own home. Quixtar offers a large number of name-brand products, plus an exclusive line of products. Quixtar's shopping categories include Home and Personal Care products, Office and Technology, Sports and Leisure, Food and Gifts, just for starters. Quixtar also provides access to a long and growing list of "partner stores."

What is a "partner store"?

It's another ecommerce company on the Internet that is partnering with Quixtar.com. From Quixtar you can link to these partner stores and shop there as well, just as you would from Quixtar's own departments. Quixtar's numerous partner stores offer everything from sportswear to groceries, toys to jewelry, software to power tools.

Is Quixtar "open" all the time?

Yes. Quixtar never closes. You can access the ordering services at Quixtar.com twenty-four hours a day, seven days a week.

Can anybody shop at the Quixtar site?
Yes. There are three ways to use the Quixtar service: as a client, a member, or an IBO.

What's a Quixtar client?
A Quixtar client has free access to the Quixtar product line and partner stores, plus information providing solutions to everyday problems—including advice from health experts, home-care specialists, and beauty consultants.

Do I have to join anything to shop at Quixtar as a client?
No.

What is a Quixtar member?
A Quixtar member enjoys discounts, promotions, buying perks, and a personalized shopping experience at Quixtar.com. Members also earn "Q credits" for many of their purchases, which can be redeemed for products, converted into frequent-flier miles, or used to get hotel and travel discounts.

When I shop from the Quixtar.com site, do I have to make a minimum order?
No.

Do I have to buy in bulk? Would I have to buy, say, a whole case of shampoo at a time?
No. You can buy just a single bottle of shampoo if you like—whatever you need.

Am I allowed to return things?
Yes. There is a Satisfaction Guaranteed policy.

What is an IBO?

IBO stands for independent business owner. A Quixtar-affiliated independent business owner enjoys all the advantages and discounts from Quixtar's online shopping service. But an IBO also has the opportunity to use Quixtar as a way to generate income.

How do they do that?

Quixtar provides a compensation plan that gives each IBO incentives to refer other people to the Quixtar site. For example, when you introduce the Quixtar.com services to people and they choose to shop from the site, you will share in the revenues that their purchases generate.

You mean, you can make money just by shopping at home from the Quixtar.com Web site and showing other people how to do it, too?

Yes.

How does Quixtar keep track of the revenues that my referrals generate?

Independent business owners have their own access code numbers. Computers track all their referrals through those code numbers so that they receive the credit.

Do the people whom I refer to Quixtar.com have to register as independent business owners?

No. They each have the same options: to access Quixtar.com as a client, a member, or an IBO.

But I still receive credit since I introduced them to the site, right?

Yes.

Let's say I refer people to Quixtar.com and they really like it, and they decide to affiliate with Quixtar as an IBO— then they introduce other people to the site. If people keep telling other people about it, is there any limit to the income I could get?

No. It's your business. Quixtar is just the tool you can use to create income. The amount you make as an IBO is up to you.

Is Quixtar basically a huge, online shopping mall?

No. Online malls are a dime a dozen. Quixtar is not a mall. Because of the personalized service and the versatility of the site, it's easier to understand Quixtar as a "Personal Shopping Portal." Quixtar.com goes way beyond a mere "mall" and is the first example of Tridigital Commerce.

"Tridigital Commerce," what is that?

Tridigital Commerce is a term used to describe the Quixtar model of business. It has three key components: Internet-based electronic commerce, member benefits, and the opportunity of business ownership through Quixtar's IBO program. Tridigital Commerce is what sets Quixtar apart from other ecommerce ventures.

Tim Foley was a famed cornerback with the Miami Dolphins. When he retired from professional sports, he spent many years as a broadcast sports announcer. As leaders of a team of Independent Business Owners that spans the globe, he and his wife, Connie, are two of the most respected, well-known, and accomplished Quixtar entrepreneurs.

Q. It seems to me that one of the biggest pluses Quixtar offers is its emphasis on bringing people together. Even with all the new technology of the Internet, Quixtar puts value on people actually meeting other people in person—not in chat rooms on the Web but face-to-face.

A. "This part of the business is so very important to what we do. That high-touch aspect is one of the things that sets Quixtar apart. You know, a lot of people think that they can just go online and sign people up strictly over the Internet, and that they're going to make hundreds of millions of dollars without any human interaction. But that's not how the Quixtar business model works.

"People are social animals. They want interaction, and they like that feeling of being involved. I think we are designed to be of service to one another, and we feel best when we're being of help to people and striving to make other peoples' lives better. That's the premise that we live on. Quixtar is based on that idea: getting out there and meeting people and talking to people and getting to know them. It's not about sitting home alone with your computer. The Internet is just a tool we use to create opportunity and build relationships. And that all depends on people coming together."

Q. Let's talk about the Development Platforms that provide Quixtar's independent business owners with the information they need to build their business.

A. "When you get started with Quixtar, you face two challenges right away. Number one is that you've never done this before. You don't really know what you need to do. It's something new. That can be intimidating, even scary, to some folks. The second thing is, as an independent business owner, you're going to build a team, and who will educate all the new IBOs who partner with your group? How do you keep the knowledge consistent? It's difficult to pass information from one person to another, because it will always change a little each time. So you have to have a mechanism in place that relays consistent, reliable information to people.

> The ultimate value with Quixtar is that you can use it to create wealth for you and your family, and achieve whatever dreams you may have in life.

"Most of the people who opt to become independent business owners with Quixtar don't do it because they have a lot of time on their hands or they're just looking for something to do. Most of them are extremely busy, very productive people. And they're looking for a way in which they can continue to work hard but have more control and reap more of the benefits. These are people who would rather see their hard work benefit themselves and their own families instead of their bosses or the owners of the companies they work for. These are very busy people. The Development Programs they have access to as IBOs are the mechanism Quixtar uses to relay that guidance and training to these busy people on a timely, regular basis.

"We all get caught up in life, and we don't have much time. Life pounds away at our emotional shores every day, and sometimes we get washed away if we don't have something there reminding us where we are going. That's what the Audio Program does; that's what the books do; and that's what the seminars do. These programs fill you with positive, encouraging information. You know, oftentimes things are happening in people's lives that aren't very encouraging or that aren't very positive; or people have habits that put them in an environment that's not encouraging. So this thing kind of pulls their heads up once in a while and lets them breathe some fresh air."

Q. Tim, you were part of the eight-member committee that helped create Quixtar. What was some of the thinking that went into that decision?

A. "It basically got down to being open and willing to change. You can't hang onto the number one spot if you're going to stay the same. You have to look at your business and say: How can we do this better? And then when you think of ways to do it better, you have to act right away because other people are improving all the time, too. You can't just sit there.

"Business is a lot like the beginning of a football season: You've got to get out there and start over again, start from scratch. You have to be willing to go to work and start over. You can't rest on your laurels or on what you did last season. You have to continue to improve and create, because other people are out there creating and working hard to get better. And the people who stop creating and innovating—their businesses will die."

Q. It's about paying attention to trends and making your move, right?

A. "Right. You have to stay ahead of the wave. And let's admit it, change is hard to accept sometimes, especially if you've already been successful at something. When you've done something the same way for awhile, and it's worked for you, it's hard to admit that you need to innovate and improve. But it's got to happen. If you want your business to survive long term, you need to adapt to change. Technologically, I'm like a lot of people. I feel further behind every day. But I know I need to move forward, embrace what's happening with the Internet, and make use of every benefit we have."

Q. There are plenty of big ecommerce companies up and running on the Internet and certainly plenty of shopping sites. How do you think Quixtar compares to these?

A. "Well, Quixtar is unique in many respects, definitely because of the high-touch aspect. I don't see any other company that offers everything we can and that brings people together like we do. We create real communities where people can actually get to know other people, not virtual, make-believe communities.

"But one thing I want to know—where is the value? You see all these big ecommerce companies out there, and venture capitalists are rushing to dump money into them. But they aren't turning a profit. At what point in time does this become a factor? How long are investors going to let companies lose money while they bet on the future? All of this money is being created, all of these Internet billionaires, but the only things of value that the investments are tied to are companies that are losing money. I don't get it. That's one element that Quixtar brings to the table: value."

Q. Before Quixtar opened its doors, whatever value ecommerce companies offered consumers seemed to be only about low prices.

A. "Right, right. And that was it. Think about it: Why would I buy from Amazon.com? Because they have the lowest price. But if they don't, then that's the end of my allegiance to Amazon. I'll just go and buy from whomever has the lowest price. But that's where the value ends—it's just about the lowest price. You see how it's been working? That's all these Internet companies, and a lot of other companies, have offered so far. There's a low price here, then one over there, then one there. And you just run around looking for the low price. Big deal. That's value?

"With Quixtar, we're not going to play that game with people. We have a totally different understanding of what value is. Value is about real convenience; it's about unique, quality products that improve your life; it's about familiar, proven brand names and the best customer service. And value is about building solid, dependable relationships between people. But value is mostly about providing an opportunity for you to benefit yourself and your family. The ultimate value with Quixtar is that you can use it to create wealth for you and your family and achieve whatever dreams you may have in life.

"Eventually all these online companies will have to follow our example and offer some real benefits besides low prices and gimmicks if they want to prosper long term. If things continue this way, you will just keep having companies that make no money. And companies that make no money, that lose hundreds of millions of dollars a year, will fall out of favor with investors. It's just a matter of time. They will have to add real value if they expect people to stay loyal to them."

A former aeronautical engineer, Jim Dornan is one of the most progressive business leaders affiliated with Quixtar. He is an integral member of the Board of Independent Business Owners and took part in the planning of Quixtar. He and his wife, Nancy, are acclaimed around the world as among the best leaders and teachers that Quixtar has to offer.

Q. Jim, what is it about Quixtar that you believe represents a quantum leap forward in business?

A. "I read recently that up to 60 percent of each dollar that consumers spend on the Internet goes toward marketing and advertising. That's amazing, almost two-thirds. That's two-thirds of every dollar going to nothing but trying to attract eyeballs. Now, in the old economy 60 to 80 percent of every dollar was spent on various middlemen: wholesalers, brokers, retailers, overhead. Nearly everything went back into distribution costs. Advertising was maybe 5 or 10 percent at the most. Now advertising has become the biggest expense because you have to somehow get customers to find your site on the Net. And the way the Net works, that is not easy. And even if they find you, who's to say they will ever come back? Consumers may have more convenience on the Internet, but they haven't necessarily gotten a better price because the money they save on middlemen is being eaten up by advertising.

But then, here we come along. Yes, we've got great convenience and service and name-brand products. But we do our advertising by word of mouth. We don't dump two-thirds of every dollar into the lap of some advertising company. We take that money and funnel it into a compensation package to pay our IBOs for their word-of-mouth referrals. It's a brilliant plan. It gives us ownership and a stake in the venture. We're not just customers. We're partners. Ecommerce may represent the new economy. But Quixtar signals the next phase of ecommerce."

> **W**e don't inject a little teamwork here and there or merely give lip service to it. Our success absolutely depends on it. A sense of community and mutual support is in everything we do.

Q. The DeVos and Van Andel families have agreed to share that wealth with each and every IBO?

A. "Right. That's how the plan works. We're not only tied in a web of personal relationships, but we are tied together economically. We shop from home on the Internet because it makes sense economically. It's convenient and it saves us money. But we also shop from Quixtar because of the compensation plan that is in place. It's a one-of-a-kind business opportunity. Stop and think about it: You get paid to shop at home over the Internet and to tell your friends about the service. It's really that simple. It's a brilliant marketing plan."

Q. And it works because it's based on the drive of individual entrepreneurs.

A. "You got it. I see Quixtar as the engine, as the technology side of it all. And that opens up a wide range of advantages and pluses that make business faster, easier, and better in so many ways. The Internet eliminates a lot of the speed bumps of business—handling orders, stocking shelves, collecting money—all the inefficient and time-consuming tasks. The Internet technology is a business enhancer.

"But the thing that puts legs under it all is the work of the teams of independent business owners. People are out there right now explaining the Internet, explaining ecommerce, explaining Quixtar. We have teams of business owners opening the door for people into the twenty-first century. It's very exciting. Those are the people who are responsible for making this thing work. And that's the key to the entire project. It's people talking to people. It's people connecting with their neighbors, their friends, and their family. We reach out one at a time and help educate people about the Internet Revolution."

Q. And the various Development Platforms that IBOs link up to are the engines that drive their businesses as well?

A. "Exactly. More than any other business environment, this is about teamwork and community. We don't inject a little teamwork here and there or merely give lip service to it. Our success absolutely depends on it. A sense of community and mutual support is in everything we do. It's there when someone is first escorted online and shown the Quixtar site. And the teamwork is there when that person goes out to develop his or her own tridigital business. They don't go alone, they go with a team to support them. Our businesses would not work without it. This is a Web-based business model, everyone is linked together in a web of support and training, for a Web-based business. But the support and community and team-building don't come through shopping from home over the Internet. They come through the training and development programs each of us plugs into.

"What we have is an opportunity for people to own their own businesses. It's cutting edge; it's the Internet; it's electronic commerce; it's the future. It's the very latest in technology. We have an exclusive digital portal, Quixtar, that offers a long list of advantages. But success in this opportunity is not based on how well you click a mouse or navigate your way through the Net. Your success is based on how well you learn to build relationships with people, face-to-face. It's based on your willingness to master people skills. In the Digital Age, using the Quixtar model of business, the better your people skills, the more relationships you create with others, the wealthier you can become.

"With our traditional business model, we were already good. But the Internet makes us better. The ecommerce model gives us all new advantages. And we make ecommerce better, because we have found a way to make a site incredibly sticky and profitable. We are doing what the other guys on the Net are scrambling to figure out how to do."

Q. Another element completely unique to Quixtar is the presence of brand-name products that people can't buy anywhere else.

A. "That's right. There are the essential shopping areas, My Home, My Health, My Self, and Hot Buys, all of which offer an exclusive product line that people will not find anywhere else on the Internet or in any brick-and-mortar store. The Quixtar site is the only place these products can be accessed. That's a tremendous plus, when it comes to understanding the advantages that we have. Take the Nutrilite vitamins, for example. Nutrilite is an incredible story. And it's the bestselling brand-name vitamin and mineral supplement on the planet. But there's only one place on the Internet where you will be able to get it, and that's at Quixtar.

"Most of the other commerce sites on the Internet sell everybody else's product line; you know, they're the mall-type sites. They're not much more than sophisticated billboards, really. They throw anything up there to get the eyeballs and then sell advertising. And that's where they make all their money.

"But not Quixtar. The people who actually shop at the site will handle the advertising through word-of-mouth referrals. That way, the DeVos and Van Andel families can concentrate on offering high-quality, brand-name, exclusive products. This exclusive product line is one of the keys to our success with Quixtar."

The Synergy of High-Touch Marketing and Twenty Other Reasons Why Quixtar.com Spells Success

S OMETIMES WHEN I find myself struggling with writer's block—which is known to occur around our house every once in a while—my wife, Alison, flies to the rescue like a superhero. "Forget everything you were trying to write or say," she says calmly. "Just clear your mind. Now, think of the one word, just one word, that best describes what you want to say to your readers. Focus on that word. Think about just that one word for awhile, without trying to write anything else. Say that word to yourself a few times. Soon that one word will take you to other words, and those words will start to thread together, and pretty soon you will be off and running again." Works like a charm every time. God bless my superhero.

At one point during the writing of this book I found myself in that situation, struggling with an idea that I couldn't quite explain. So Alison challenged me. I'll never forget the moment. We were sitting on the front porch, watching our cat Jack patter across the lawn. I was talking about how I couldn't find the right words to explain something, and Alison looked right at me and asked: "What is the one word that sums up Quixtar? I've heard you go on for weeks about how great Quixtar is. But if you had to boil it all down to just one word, what would that word be? What is it all about in just one word?"

Hmm . . . Quixtar in just one word. I started with some initial ideas: ecommerce, network, value, opportunity, convenience, potential, progressive, versatile, wow! But none of these words really summed up all the subtleties of Quixtar. And then a little later, it hit me—the one word that perfectly sums up what Quixtar is all about is *synergy*.

Plainly put, synergy means to work together. It describes the way that different and distinct agencies, businesses, or individuals act jointly, producing a total effect that is far greater than the mere sum of their parts. Synergy describes a network of actions and accomplishment. Quixtar is a synergistic, high-tech, high-touch process built on many mutually beneficial relationships. The more I thought about it, the more I realized that synergy is the key to understanding what makes the Quixtar model of business truly exceptional.

In this chapter we will look at what makes Quixtar really work, as a business, as an opportunity, and as an on- and offline community. We'll start with the synergy that underlies the entire venture, then look at twenty other reasons why Quixtar.com spells success.

Understanding the Quixtar Synergy

QUIXTAR'S SYNERGY RELIES on the ongoing creation and nurturing of numerous alliances. First, there is an array of partnering corporations, manufacturers, and stores that provides products, services, and information for distribution through the Quixtar.com Web site. Second, a vast infrastructure consolidates the orders, makes sure all the items get where they are supposed to go, and ensures that good service is consistently maintained. Third, there are technical teams that build, maintain, and constantly update and improve the Quixtar Web site. And fourth is the web of millions of independent business owners, members, clients, and net surfers who link up with Quixtar.com each day.

> . . . the one word that perfectly sums up what Quixtar is all about is *synergy.*

It is in this last category where the impressive Quixtar synergy is most evident—particularly among the networks of IBOs and business leaders. These men and women, *working together* toward individual and common goals, are responsible for making Quixtar one of the true wonders of the Internet Revolution.

Quixtar.com is an impressive Web site, but it would not be the ecommerce success story that it is without these organizations and teams of business leaders. These entrepreneurs integrate Quixtar into their lives and share its advantages with others. Demonstrating the synergy at work, Quixtar.com owes much of its success to their hard work. And in turn, they can credit their individual achievements in part to the opportunities that Quixtar provides.

IN A TRADITIONAL networking business of the twentieth century, distributors in the field recruited and sponsored direct-sales people to use and sell products. In the twenty-first-century

Quixtar model, there are no distributors, there is no field, and recruiting becomes an obsolete concept.

Since people shop at home over the Internet, products and services are sent directly to each consumer who accesses Quixtar.com—whether that person is an IBO, a member, or a client. There is no personal distribution required—no stocking the garage with inventory, no "product pickup," no trunkful of items that you have to deliver to someone across town. As a result, there are no "distributors."

As one Quixtar leader told me: "I don't distribute products anymore. That's the old model. With Quixtar, people can access the products themselves over the Internet, order whatever they want, and have it sent directly to their front door. I don't have to take them their toothpaste or Poptarts or motor oil. Quixtar handles all of that for me. I'm free now to focus on what's really important: building relationships with people."

In the twenty-first-century Quixtar model, the concept of a "field" of distributors is also done away with. The notion is a remnant of the days when a company would send its salespeople out to drum up business and move products. But with Quixtar, there is no field of "reps" or salesmen. Instead, a web of independent business owners, taking advantage of various Development Platforms, agree to partner with Quixtar in a mutually beneficial, contractual arrangement.

In this new synergy each element is as important as any other. There is no "company on the hill" that sends forth its "army of salespeople" into the world. There is instead a web of independent companies, each standing atop its own hill. The Quixtar model introduces a novel component of equality that raises referral marketing to a new level. In fact, given

the flexibility of Tridigital Commerce, referral-based marketing has become just one part of the entire Quixtar equation.

INSTEAD OF "RECRUITING" distributors—again, a
remnant of the days of multilevel marketing—the success of
Quixtar.com is based on the dynamics of Tridigital Commerce, which combine:

1. Internet-based electronic commerce,
2. Member benefits—an exclusive shopping experience,
   and
3. An IBO opportunity—the Internet's ultimate affiliate program.

Up-front, face-to-face recommendations, the sharing of
information, and word-of-mouth referrals take the place of
older recruiting techniques. This is an important point that
many people unfamiliar with the new Quixtar model may
miss. With multiple avenues of possible participation, there
are many ways to benefit from the Personal Shopping Portal
at Quixtar.com besides registering as an independent business owner. The spectrum of Tridigital Commerce opens up
new options that far surpass the capabilities of the old referral-based marketing strategy.

One independent business owner described it to me like
this: "I'd pass out catalogs under the old model, then I went
out and tried to get people to sign up in a business. And that
wasn't easy. It could be done, sure, but it wasn't easy. Some
people would quit because they didn't want to stick it out
and do the work. But Quixtar's all about options. It's totally
different. You still have to work, don't get me wrong, but
with all the options it makes things so different.

"When I sit down to tell someone about Quixtar.com, I can give them all sorts of choices now. The goal is to take advantage of what Quixtar has to offer—shopping at home over the Internet, super deals, great products, home delivery, member benefits, personalized service, even the IBO opportunity. But how you take advantage of all that is up to you. My job is to just lay out all the choices you have. I'm not there to get people into anything. I'm there to show them the hottest thing in ecommerce and then sketch out different ways that they can benefit from it."

TRIDIGITAL COMMERCE, WHICH makes the Quixtar IBO opportunity so versatile, is one-third high-tech and two-thirds high-touch. It is one part Internet-based commerce combined with two parts face-to-face, personable interaction. It is this formula of Tridigital Commerce that helps make the Quixtar approach truly unique and powerful in the new economy.

Helping to oversee the client, member, and IBO registration process, individual sponsors serve as key development partners and as consultants for all those who are new to the network. As a bridge of communication, each individual development partner is crucial to the viability of the web. Communication, support, and teaching are the triad upon which the synergy among the IBOs depends.

One important point: in the twentieth-century networking model, an individual might have been said to be "in Amway." But given the Quixtar.com strategy, there is nothing for the independent business owner to be "in," so that concept falls away. An IBO cannot be said to be "in" Quixtar, since Quixtar.com is simply a Personal Shopping Portal on the World Wide Web. Put it this way: We do not think of a new McDonald's franchisee as being "in" McDonald's. Similarly, it makes no sense to say that an IBO is "in" Quixtar.

"Primarily, what we are doing is empowering the individual," says entrepreneur and well-known Quixtar leader Jody Victor, "by providing him or her with the benefits of a totally unique, online order consolidation service, which is Quixtar. You have an opportunity to get into business for yourself, set yourself up as an independent business owner, and you will be *powered* by Quixtar.com. Quixtar is not the business. Quixtar is a magnificent, one-of-a-kind site on the Internet. But it's not the business. It's the digital engine that *powers* your own business."

RESPONSIBLE FOR MUCH of Quixtar's synergy are a number of IBO Development Platforms. Each Development Platform is created and provided by an incorporated organization of accomplished Quixtar business leaders. Independent business owners use these Development Platforms to build their Tridigital marketing teams.

A business needs a formula for success—something to rest on, a foundation. The Quixtar-affiliated businesses are built on these IBO Development Platforms.

Each platform is made up of a number of programs that provide the knowledge, guidance, and materials that IBOs need to build their businesses. These teaching programs include personalized instruction, audio files, regular readings, and ecommerce seminars.

An IBO Development Platform is like an operating system, similar to Microsoft's "Windows." If you open "Windows," you will notice that it contains a lot of different computer programs that you can use—like Word, PowerPoint, Excel, or Access. All of these individual programs are included within the "Windows" platform. The platform pulls all those programs together in one convenient package.

The IBO Development Platforms operate in the same way—only instead of helping someone use a computer, they help someone build a business. An IBO Development Platform pulls together all the instructional programs and design strategies that independent business owners need to build successful, Web-based companies.

An IBO Development Platform is a multimedia experience—offering on- and offline instructional programs. Each organization of Quixtar leaders also hosts Internet portals—sites on the World Wide Web that are like community gathering places. IBOs use these portals to stay in touch with each other online, to access the Quixtar.com Web site, and to stay up-to-date on the latest program information.

Quixtar's high-touch aspect—one of the principle virtues that sets it apart from all other ecommerce ventures—does not necessarily come from the Quixtar.com Web site itself. Rather, the high-touch experience stems from the work of the IBO Development Platforms. It is this high-touch personalization that makes the marketing synergy so powerful.

Twenty Other Reasons Why Quixtar.com Spells Success

THE SYNERGY OF high-touch marketing—rooted in the dynamics of the IBO Development Platforms—is the foremost reason why Quixtar.com promises to be one of the most prosperous ventures to spring from the Internet Revolution. But there are many other important factors that play to Quixtar's advantage. Let's take a look at some.

1. Taking Advantage of Trends

Remember one of the key factors that propelled McDonald's to the top of the restaurant and franchise business: being at the vanguard of change. That progressiveness is absolutely critical to making a business venture really take off. Entrepreneurs and companies that learn best how to anticipate and quickly take advantage of cultural and economic trends will be the success stories of tomorrow. The Quixtar.com model is perfectly positioned to capitalize on four exploding trends of the new economy.

The first is a boom in computer sales. As prices for computer systems and software continue to plummet, and speed and ability improve, industry analysts estimate that over 100 million personal computers will be sold in 1999 alone. More than that will likely be sold the following year. It won't be long before people are buying more computers than television sets. The personal computer is fast becoming a standard household appliance, just like a stove or a refrigerator.

The second trend is the growth in the use of the Internet. I don't believe it's at all unreasonable to expect that over one billion people will be online and over one hundred million Web sites will be posted by the year 2020 or even sooner. The Internet will play an increasing part in the daily lives of more and more people around the world. As I write this book, screens with Internet access are being installed on exercise equipment, at highway rest stops, in automobiles, in restaurants, and at gas pumps.

The third trend Quixtar will certainly benefit from is the boom in online shopping—which is forecasted to grow from about $8 billion in 1999 to well over $100 billion by the year 2003. Does this mean all retail stores will one day close? Probably not. Some of them, perhaps as much as a third, might shut down. The rest will likely replace their employee-operated cash registers with Web-access kiosks where purchases will be made. The items we want to buy would then be shipped from a regional warehouse to our home address. Of course, stores and shopping will still exist as the Digital Age unfolds. But their form and function will change—because nearly everything we now leave our homes to buy will one day be available online.

> **P**lainly put, synergy means to work together. It describes the way that different and distinct agencies, businesses, or individuals act jointly, producing a total effect that is far greater than the mere sum of their parts.

The fourth great trend of the new economy that Quixtar takes advantage of is the sharp rise in the number of home-based businesses. The number of people working at home in the United States jumped from 4 million in 1990 to almost 16 million by the year 2000. An *American Demographics* magazine cover story in June of 1999 reported: "With telecommuting finally taking hold and people starting home businesses at a rate of 2 million a year, with technology turning households into telecommunications centers and flexibility becoming the war cry among workers not only coast to coast but worldwide, home business is big business. And it's expected to get even bigger in the millennium."

Quixtar is right on time, complete with a paperless, personalized, continually updated "virtual office" that each of its independent business owners utilizes. The Internet Revolution is ushering in a new era of digital cottage industries, where we will have the opportunity to work at home as people did before the Industrial and Corporate Revolutions.

2. Disintermediation

Beginning in the early 1800s, the Industrial Revolution changed the way that products were distributed to consumers by replacing a cottage industry of home-based craftspeople with regional networks of shopkeepers and mercantile stores. Just about one hundred years after that, the Corporate Revolution replaced the mercantile networks with traveling salesman, mail-order catalogs, and franchised stores. Here at the dawn of the twenty-first century, the Internet Revolution is changing that distribution network yet again.

A by-product from the boom of online shopping, "disintermediation"—getting rid of the middleman—has become one of the new buzz words of ecommerce. In his 1999 book *Business @ The Speed of Thought*, Microsoft CEO Bill Gates described it like this: "Now that customers can deal directly with manufacturing and service providers, there is little value added in simply transferring goods or information. Various commentators have predicted 'the death of the middleman.' Certainly, the value of a pass-through middleman is quickly falling to zero. . . . If you're a middleman, the Internet's promise of cheaper prices and faster service can 'disintermediate' you, eliminate your role of assisting in the transaction between the producer and the customer."

For decades now, the DeVos and Van Andel families and their partnering business leaders have pioneered disintermediation in business-to-consumer commerce by building referral networks of in-home shoppers and distributors. They have taken that formula and experience to a new, high-tech level with Quixtar.com. By replacing middlemen with an online Personal Shopping Portal, Quixtar, the consumer reaps the rewards and benefits that Internet disintermediation can offer.

The money that used to go to middlemen and wholesale brokers now goes to members, through discounts and specials, and to IBOs, through an incentive-based referral program.

3. New Technology/New Business Model

Do you remember the "Secret Formula" that made the Industrial and Corporate Revolutions such powerful agents for change? It was this: Emerging technologies were combined with new ways of doing business. We saw it with Arkwright's factory system, which was built around new textile looms. We saw it with the pyramid-shaped bureaucracy of the corporation, which was combined with new office machines. And we are witnessing the same process take place in the Internet Revolution as entrepreneurs explore the money-making possibilities of the online world.

A number of business models have been created for ecommerce. Consider Amazon.com's Digital Age bookstore, ebay's success with instant auctions, Yahoo's runaway hit as a portal and cyber hub, or AOL's masterful achievements as a virtual community. Add to this growing list of new business models the high-tech, high-touch Tridigital Commerce of Quixtar.com.

Seema Williams is an analyst on the Consumer Ecommerce Research Team at Forrester Research. I asked her what she thought about the Quixtar business model. "Quixtar is a fabulous idea," she replied. "It's absolutely the right thing at the right time. Quixtar takes a conventional, offline business model, adapts it to the Internet, and creates something new in the process. And what's really going to work in their favor is the fact that the online environment is perfect for what they're doing."

4. The Quixtar Product Line

One of the keys to the future of online shopping is a Web site's ability to offer a diverse range of products. Sure, you can rake in a lot of revenue just selling books—Amazon.com has proven that. But now Amazon offers toys, clothes, computers, and more. As people become accustomed to buying over the Internet, they will be seeking a one-stop, all-in-one-shopping-cart experience. It's the same approach that made one-stop brick-and-mortar stores like WalMart and K-Mart so successful.

Who wants to go to one site to buy breakfast cereal, another to buy socks, another to purchase paper towels, and still another to buy dog food—each one a separate transaction with different delivery costs?

As a consolidated ordering service, Quixtar.com is a one-stop Personal Shopping Portal that makes all those various stops and starts obsolete. It brings together a wide array of familiar, brand-name products and services into one Web location. With its exclusive, name-brand products, and online partner stores all in place, Quixtar is well-equipped to lead the way in online retailing.

David Rush is a principal with Kurt Salmon Associates, one of the world's top management consulting firms serving the retail and consumer products industries. "What we're looking at now are changing buying habits," he explained during an interview. "And we're going to see a lot more of it in the next few years. Today I stop by the local drugstore or grocery for whatever I need. But in tomorrow's Quixtar world it will be standard operating procedure to click on the Net and order all those products, then have them sent right to my home. The Quixtar model has phenomenal potential."

Tridigital Commerce, which makes the Quixtar IBO opportunity so versatile, is one-third high-tech and two-thirds high-touch. It is one part Internet-based commerce combined with two parts face-to-face, personable interaction. It is this formula of Tridigital Commerce that helps make the Quixtar approach truly unique and powerful in the new economy.

5. DeVos and Van Andel Families

One of Quixtar's strongest assets is the support that it enjoys from the company's founding families. The DeVos and Van Andel families consistently rank among America's wealthiest families. They offer an incredibly solid financial footing to support the Quixtar venture. All of the business leaders affiliated with Quixtar.com whom I interviewed for this book commented on the good fortune they have to be partnering with these two families.

Not only do they have the capital to make sure that Quixtar.com is the Internet's premiere digital destination, but the DeVos and Van Andel families benefit from two generations of phenomenally successful business experience. As one Quixtar leader told me: "How many multi-billion dollar companies do people need to build before you realize they have what it takes? The DeVos and Van Andel families don't need to prove anything to me. I couldn't think of any finer, more experienced, more capable people to be in business with."

6. Dot Com Thinking

As you read in a previous chapter, Quixtar.com has its historical roots in the referral-based marketing industry of the twentieth century. For decades the DeVos and Van Andel families and their affiliated business leaders pioneered that marketing strategy and used it to create teams of entrepreneurs that now span the globe. Here at the dawn of the Digital Age, we can look back now and see that their novel way of doing business was very much ahead of its time. Long before Internet-based ecommerce even existed, they demonstrated what I like to call "dot com thinking."

"These guys were operating like there was a World Wide Web, even before there was a Web," Quixtar leader Andy Andrews said. "All these companies could come to them with no advertising costs and have instant access to a loyal customer base of home shoppers. When you think about it, the conventional business model was like an ecommerce Web site, except they used printed catalogs and called in their orders on the phone. No matter where you were, you could plug into this network and order products and go shopping right from your house. I look at the way online shopping works and I think, they've already been doing this for years!"

Brad Doyle, Quixtar leader and co-founder of the Technology Development Group, agrees that the DeVos and Van

Andel families pioneered dot com thinking a long time ago. "That's a big reason why Quixtar is so promising," he told me. "From a business standpoint, we've been operating like this for over forty years. In the 1950s and 1960s we taught people how to get products and services in an alternative way by delivering them to their door. In the '70s and '80s we brought people products through a direct-selling party plan. And in the '90s we perfected the catalog distribution business. Now we've taken all that experience and used it to create a new business model for the Internet. If there's any group in the world that knows how to teach people how to change their buying habits and shop from home, it's us."

Dot com thinking—as opposed to a traditional, bricks-and-mortar paradigm—has been at the heart of the DeVos and Van Andel families' approach to business since they were Nutrilite distributors in the 1940s. Over the last fifty-plus years they and their leaders fine-tuned a marketing strategy that relied on personal, face-to-face referrals—not on bill-boards, radio ads, or any other customary advertising methods. And they have taught people, one household at a time, alternative ways to access products and services they would normally go to a store to buy. In a way, the DeVos and Van Andel families created the first truly successful cyber-company. They were cyber before cyber was cool.

During my interview with Seema Williams of Forrester Research, I asked her to what extent she thought those decades of dot com thinking would benefit Quixtar. Without hesitation, she said: "Knowing what we know now, I think the DeVos and Van Andel families were way ahead of their time. The business leaders who bring that experience to

Quixtar are ahead of the curve. They've already mastered what every other Internet-based retailer is trying to figure out. The Quixtar model was totally made for this medium."

7. Advanced Infrastructure

As a direct result of their decades of dot com thinking, the DeVos and Van Andel families have invested quite heavily in building an infrastructure to support their network of three million in-home consumers around the world. They already have 14,000 employees in place and ready to go, 61 distribution warehouses around the world, plus 11 automated regional service centers throughout North America—one of which was named the 1998 Warehouse of the Year by *Warehousing Management* magazine. They have the ability to take a product order for any item and deliver it in two to five days to the front doorsteps of about two-thirds of the world's population.

"The good news is that we already have the infrastructure to do this very well," Dave Van Andel told *Business 2.0* magazine in August of 1999. "We've had our distribution network in place for thirty-five years, with distribution centers strategically located throughout the country. We also have a catalog operation, with customer-service operators. We have the ability to ship via UPS and FedEx. Plus, we have the ability to quickly mainstream new products into that distribution channel."

From the moment it went online, Quixtar.com has benefited from that advanced, automated infrastructure. Nearly every other Web-based company that aims to take orders and deliver products to the booming online shopping population is scrambling to catch up with Quixtar.

8. Premium Customer Service

Gene DeRose is the CEO and chairman of New York–based Jupiter Communications, one of the world's top research and consulting firms for businesses that use emerging digital technologies. I asked him about the current state of customer service at ecommerce Web sites. "It's the singular thing we think has been most overlooked so far," he said flatly.

According to Jupiter's research, nearly half of the leading, most successful Web sites have substandard customer service. A recent Jupiter survey found that many popular sites take longer than five days to return e-mail. Some do not even offer an e-mail address, and most do not even give their customers a telephone number to call.

A February 1999 study by Shelley Taylor & Associates found that one out of four online stores fail to provide a navigation guide to help customers get around their virtual stores. Another study discovered that 67 percent of attempted online purchases end in no-sales because of poor or nonexistent customer service.

"Most of the Internet is just not very customer-friendly yet," DeRose admitted. "A lot of companies have a long way to go. It can be done, but there's a lot of work to do."

Enter Quixtar. Quixtar.com's clients, members, and IBOs benefit from a superb, easy-to-navigate Web site, where all prices, policies, and standards are clearly marked—including a Satisfaction Guaranteed policy. They can also turn to an extended hours, 1-800 phone bank where hundreds of people are available to answer questions and provide guidance and assistance. Should they prefer more personalized customer service, they could contact the Quixtar-affiliated IBO who referred them to the site. No other destination on the Internet offers this degree of personal interaction and service.

9. *Tridigital Communities*

One of the new mantras for the Digital Age will be: Create Community. Civic life in America is at an all-time low, and people feel increasingly isolated from one another. Building community and stepping up our relationships with others will be a priority in the new millennium.

In his insightful study of the new economy, *Webonomics,* author Evan Schwartz writes: "The concept of community is one of the main themes that recurs in Webonomics. . . . Contrary to what some people believe, the Web is not a *mass* medium. It's a niche medium, a personal medium, and an interactive medium." In other words, the Internet is all about bringing people together. It's about people enriching their lives by building relationships with others. That's what the engineers at ARPA had in mind when they first started investigating computer networking in the 1960s. And that's what Tim Berners-Lee was thinking when he created the World Wide Web program: facilitating the process that brings people together.

Building communities is at the very core of what Quixtar.com is all about. Thanks to Quixtar's Tridigital marketing approach—which combines the Internet with real life, in-person communication—creating new relationships occurs both on- and offline. Remember one of the great lessons from the history of innovation? *It's not about the machine.* The Internet Revolution is not about computers or transistors or online shopping. It's about people, their families, their hopes and dreams; it's about the relationships we have with one another.

Quixtar business leader Jody Victor emphasized the creation of Tridigital communities during my interview with him. "It not about the corporation anymore. It's about the individual. It's all about building teams, mentoring others, serving others. It's about personalization and relationships. It's about family and trust. It's about believing and achieving. With our opportunity, you're going to see live rooms, not chat rooms. We're going to fill the largest coliseums throughout the United States and Canada."

10. Achievement-Oriented Team Building

Quixtar's high-tech, high-touch marketing model uses the very latest digital technologies to create long-lasting relationships among people—creating new connections both on- and offline. But it takes a leadership-based strategy to actually put that model to work. That's where the IBO Development Platforms come into play.

The IBO Development Platforms provide those important teaching and support programs that make it possible to build the teams that make up the Tridigital Communities. The Development Platforms personalize the Quixtar experience for each and every independent business owner. In their mission to cultivate leaders and entrepreneurs, the Development Platforms also teach success principles that are rarely if ever taught in schools.

Quixtar leader Bert Gulick explained it to me this way: "Success in life, in anything—business, sports, the arts, you name it—depends not just on gaining the right knowledge and being able to plug into the right information source, it depends on how well you make use of the right attitudes— things like integrity, loyalty, and persistence. And you don't develop integrity, persistence, or loyalty by just educating someone about business techniques. You've got to provide more than that. The way you learn a certain attitude that's going to make

you better at business, and a better person overall, is to immerse yourself in an environment where people share those
attitudes—where great value is placed on integrity, persistence,
and loyalty. These qualities are not always valued in the corporate world, but with those of us who affiliate with Quixtar,
they are central to what we do. Developing those attitudes and
qualities are critical to the teaching and support programs that
we offer our independent business owners."

   A success-driven, team-building experience, oriented
around both personal and group achievement, is usually re-
served for professional athletes. But Quixtar.com's affiliated
IBO leaders have found a way to integrate that dynamic into
a winning business model. Like any all-star team, the IBO
leaders have found a way to blend personal expression and
talents into a proven pattern of success.

11. Win-Win Together

One of the first things that companies realize as they make the
transition to a digital environment is that they cannot go it
alone anymore. The rules have changed. The Corporate Revolution gave us a way of doing business that dominated much
of twentieth-century culture and society. Independence and
self-reliance were top corporate values. Asking for help was a
sign of weakness. Relying on others was a crutch. You only
won if the other guy lost. But all of that is rapidly becoming
history, as we watch the old corporate way of doing things
slowly erode. In the Digital Age things work differently.

   "Want to really benefit from ecommerce?" *Business 2.0*
magazine asked its readers in a September 1999 article. "Better
rethink the way your company operates." The story's authors described the old business model as an "organizational

environment that is hierarchically fixed and politically segmented—one where fiefdoms drive attitudes. Having been trained in the traditional hierarchical paradigm, we learn to work within strict lines and to focus on optimizing our individual part without concern for the whole."

Compared to the conventional business paradigm, the authors continued, the Internet "is radically different. Internet culture is agile, fast-paced, and highly receptive to new solutions. Its architecture is open and fluid; it is grounded in networked relationships and affiliations."

Jupiter Communication's Gene DeRose emphasized that point as well: "This is a relationship-driven industry. The importance of relationships and partnerships right up and down the line—this is the key to it all. It's a whole new science of business. Nobody can do it alone anymore."

One of the things that makes Quixtar.com a success is the fact that this philosophy is a touchstone of the shared belief system of every IBO affiliated with the venture. But even more than that, it is exactly how the Quixtar.com business model succeeds in the first place: Personal success depends on how well you can create relationships, build teams, and help others achieve. It is a win-win-together approach to business that dovetails perfectly with the way things work in the new digital environment.

"As we enter the twenty-first century," Quixtar leader Brian Hays explained, "I think the key to success in anything, certainly business, will be the creation of personal relationships. That has become a priority now more than ever before. Quixtar brings that dimension to ecommerce, far ahead of any other company out there. The Quixtar model of business allows us to work side-by-side with people, not only on the Net, but in real life as well."

Quixtar entrepreneur and teacher Jim Dornan put it this way: "A sense of community and mutual support is in everything we do. It's there when someone is first escorted online and shown the Quixtar site. And the teamwork is there when that person goes out to develop his or her own Tridigital business. They don't go alone, they go with a team to support them. Our businesses would not work without it. This is a Web-based business model—everyone is linked together in a web of support and training—for a Web-based business."

A by-product from the boom of online shopping, "disintermediation"— getting rid of the middleman—has become one of the new buzz words of ecommerce.

Creating alliances, building relationships, benefiting from the experience and wisdom of others, focusing on the success of your partnerships, and helping others succeed—these are the new principles of business for the twenty-first century.

12. Agile and Fast-Paced

Another unique advantage that Quixtar's high-tech, high-touch model brings to the Web is an outstanding proficiency to swiftly adapt to change. That ability will be a great asset in the fast-paced new world of business. In fact, companies will not achieve any measure of success without it. It's like the saying goes: The only constant is change. That is the song of the new millennium.

As Evan Schwartz writes in *Webonomics:* "Rapid change is the only sure thing about the future of technology. The people who first figure out how to best take advantage of these changes will generate enormous value for themselves and their customers. Those who don't spot these opportunities will be left under water. In the end, only the agile will survive."

"You have to be nimble," Gene DeRose counseled. "You want to have a company that succeeds with digital technology? Then you have to be constantly on the move, constantly aware of what's going on, and constantly ready to adapt to changing conditions. Because conditions and technology are changing all the time."

Since Quixtar's affiliated business owners are all linked together by an on- and offline communication network, they have the ability to respond as one unit almost instantly. IBOs are each plugged into a common voicemail system, e-mail, and training system, and receive regular updates through their Web portals. The cohesiveness is remarkable. And that community of communication gives the entire Quixtar network the ability to turn on a dime.

13. Affiliate-Referral Advertising

Quixtar's Tridigital approach offers another element that has proven to be advantageous in ecommerce: affiliate-referral advertising. Applying what they learned with their previous networking success, Quixtar's business leaders have brought to the Internet a referral-marketing program that was tailor-made for the cyber environment.

Advertising for Internet-based businesses—what some people in the industry call "attracting eyeballs"—has proven to be a real challenge. "If you look at some of the ecommerce start-ups in the early days," David Rush of Kurt Salmon Associates explained, "you see that marketing on the Web itself was the big trend in advertising. Everybody thought they could throw up a few banner ads and get rich. But what they found over time is that the click through rate—the number of people who actually click on a banner ad and come through to your site—was actually very low. So they've started pouring their money into traditional marketing."

According to Competitive Media Reporting, the amount that Web-based companies spent on offline advertising—like billboards, radio, and television ads—has soared 452 percent, to almost $600 million in 1998. The online discount broker E*Trade has already invested more than $100 million into advertising just to get eyeballs to its site.

Instead of sinking tens or hundreds of millions of revenue dollars into television ads and radio spots, Quixtar.com takes a different tack. The company uses that money to compensate its affiliated independent business owners for word-of-mouth advertising. This method is extremely rewarding.

A recent survey found that online shoppers are more likely to spread the word about a great consumer Web site than they are about movies or restaurants. The Opinion Research Corporation International discovered that "the typical Internet consumer tells twelve additional people about his or her online shopping experience"—versus the typical consumer who tells nine people about a favorite film and six people about a good restaurant. Simply put, word-of-mouth referrals are the life-blood of a successful Web site.

"These online shopping communities don't build themselves," Quixtar leader Jim Floor told me. "You will either spend a large fortune, most of your income, on advertising;

or you will have to compensate people for word-of-mouth referrals. We prefer the human touch."

"Yes, we've got great convenience and service and name-brand products," well-known Quixtar entrepreneur Jim Dornan commented. "But we do our advertising by word-of-mouth. We don't dump two-thirds of every dollar into the lap of some advertising company. We take that money and funnel it into a compensation package to pay our IBOs for their word-of-mouth referrals. It's a brilliant plan. It gives us ownership and a stake in the venture. We're not just customers. We're partners. Ecommerce may represent the new economy. But Quixtar signals the next phase of ecommerce."

"I am totally impressed by the Quixtar approach," industry analyst David Rush declared. "I personally believe it's going to be much more effective than any traditional advertising approach has been. They've developed a remarkable formula that helps people help themselves. A Quixtar IBO has every incentive in the world to share Quixtar's services with friends, co-workers, and anyone they know or might meet. Most of them will be shopping at home over the Internet at some point anyway. Why not plug into a site that pays them to shop there? The referral compensation plan is a great benefit for Quixtar as a company in terms of the operational costs. And at the same time, an IBO enjoys the full commission benefits. Everybody wins."

14. Trustworthy Consumer Information

Another advantage Quixtar enjoys is its built-in capability to offer personalized consumer advice and product information—something the online shopping community is in need of. Quixtar can take that information to people—not through an anonymous mass medium like television or radio—but directly through friends and family and via people we already know and trust.

"As the Web becomes an infinite supply of goods and services," one *New York Times* ecommerce article reads, "people crave guidance on what and where to buy. So far, the great number of online shopping guides present quantitative machine-sorted and machine-generated data: comparisons of product prices and specifications. But what consumers need is a recommendation that gets beyond that: the advice of someone they trust, someone just like them."

Every day we are bombarded by a profusion of commercials and promotions—buy this product, wear that shirt, drive this car. It gets to be downright unbearable sometimes. What we need is advice from people we already trust or from people we readily identify with. As we move into the new millennium, we will be looking for consumer advice and product knowledge through personalized mediums—not from a one-size-fits-all, mass-market TV ad. That's where Quixtar's high-tech, high-touch marketing model leads the way.

According to Jupiter's research, nearly half of the leading, most successful Web sites have substandard customer service.

15. Tradition of Teaching

One of the things of which the Internet Revolution has reminded us is that just when you think you know something, along comes something new to learn. But assimilating new technologies and innovations into our lives is not always a frictionless event. Sometimes it can be particularly challenging.

As a friend of mine joked the other day: "How do they expect me to figure out e-mail when I have trouble opening a child-proof cap?"

To its advantage, Quixtar.com offers a vast network of business owners, each of whom is equipped to take people by the hand and help them figure out how to make this world of new technology work for them. It is a long tradition of teaching that began with Nutrilite Products.

Rich DeVos and Jay Van Andel represented Nutrilite vitamins at a time when most Americans had probably never even heard of a vitamin supplement. It was their job to educate people, one household at a time, about the benefits and rewards that come from preventive health care. When they began offering concentrated, biodegradable cleaning products, it's likely they had to explain those terms to most of their customers as well. That tradition of helping people, one-on-one, understand and learn how to benefit from unfamiliar innovations has been carried forth into the Digital Age, where it will become a supremely valuable asset.

"People need help with all this stuff," Quixtar leader Bill Florence said. "Ask all of the people who've learned to turn on a computer and get on the Internet: Chances are someone sat there with them and showed them how to do it. Someone was there to answer their questions and show them the way. I think that's a big part about what we are doing. People are out there right now teaching and leading and showing others the way. They're helping people do things they didn't know they could do. The more that these new technologies become a part of our lives, the more people will need someone there to take the time and help them learn. That's the most rewarding thing about what we're doing: seeing people realize that they can do it, that they are capable. I can't tell you how great it is to watch someone succeed whom you've helped get there. It's the best thing about what we do."

And as Quixtar entrepreneur Bert Gulick told me: "We have the opportunity to actually introduce the Internet *and* Quixtar together, at the same time, to people. We will be the global, grassroots education process that brings millions of people into the twenty-first century. It's really amazing how it all comes together. We have now an incentive, a reward for actually taking the time to teach our neighbors how to get to the Internet and add value and convenience to their lives. No other company on the Internet offers a program like this. It is truly unique."

16. Demographics

Another reason why Quixtar.com spells success is because of the demographics of those who have already taken advantage of the service. All indications are that the spectrum of people who are affiliated with Quixtar—either as clients, members, or business owners—will greatly contribute to the success of the venture.

"If you take a look at the people we've already registered," Quixtar leader and board member Brad Doyle told me, "you'll see that we've got demographics that are three times more likely to be online; we have more education than the average American and more income than the average American. Before Quixtar, we built in-home shopping networks through catalogs. The demographics of a catalog buyer are identical to those of the early adopters of Internet technology. So we are those pioneers who traditionally bring massive numbers of people into any new technology." These demographics also make Quixtar's Tridigital community appealing to manufacturers and service providers who are eager to access the new online shopping market.

Ann Stephens is the president of PC Data, a northern Virginia–based research firm that tracks Internet commerce, Web activity, and point-of-sale statistics. "It's all about the value of your customer base," she explained during an interview. "What are their demographics? What's impressive to us is the percentage of people who buy from that site versus the percentage who just go there. The demographics of the people who bought from that site, and how loyal they are—if they come back every week and every month and keep buying. That is all valuable information that helps us access how a commercial site is doing. If those things don't happen, it's not especially valuable. It's just another site."

But even more than that, it is exactly how the Quixtar.com business model succeeds in the first place: Personal success depends on how well you can create relationships, build teams, and help others achieve. It is a win-win-together approach to business that dovetails perfectly with the way things work in the new digital environment.

But if it does happen, as is the case of Quixtar.com, then you've got an ecommerce success story. Quixtar's demographics reveal loyal, educated, Web-savvy, motivated online consumers.

17. The Alliance Factor

On September 1, 1999, Quixtar.com introduced the World Wide Web's premiere loyalty program. Ecommerce analysts would be hard-pressed to find another site that offers its affiliates as much potential as this one. "With Quixtar," Andy Andrews observed, "you're not just a faceless customer on the Web, you're a partner. You're an independent business owner, and your success is Quixtar's success. We're all working together. It's your store, your Web site. You get a piece of everything you buy. You get a piece of everything you refer."

Finding ways to attract Internet surfers has proven to be a costly task. The well-known destinations on the Web are shelling out millions of dollars to attract all those "eyeballs." But creating a community of loyal, online shoppers who will return again and again has been the greatest challenge. Gene DeRose of Jupiter Communications calls the loyalty issue "the single most important thing on the Internet."

Quixtar leader Brian Hays explained: "We bring an aspect to the table that no other company in the entire world has the ability to do—a loyal base. The main thing that ecommerce companies are struggling with is how to attract and keep traffic; how to increase the eyeballs and the stick power. Quixtar comes to the Net with a community of over a million people ready to support the launch. Where most companies are starting from a zero foundation, we already have a million highly motivated entrepreneurs who recognize the trend of ecommerce and are anxious to create their own Internet business using the Quixtar model."

By generously compensating its independent business owners for their referrals, Quixtar.com has fashioned an ingenious loyalty program that works extremely well. Independent Business Owners who learn how to develop Tridigital marketing teams have the opportunity to create real wealth for themselves and their families.

Analysts and writers who cover the Internet industry often refer to a Web site's degree of loyalty among its visitors as its level of "stickiness"—sticky Web sites manage to bring people back again and again, while unsticky sites do not. In the Web world, the logic goes, it's good to be sticky.

I must be honest, though; I have never really cared for the term *sticky*. It makes all us Internet surfers sound like flies or insects and makes excellent Web sites sound like nothing but fly paper. In the case of Quixtar's IBO program, I don't even believe the term adequately applies to what's really going on.

If I am a loyal online shopper to a certain Web site, then we could say that site is sticky—it brings me back again and again. But Quixtar.com's IBO program goes beyond the idea of a regular customer. The IBO paradigm is best understood as a partnering agreement between two businesses. Quixtar and the affiliated independent business owner have joined in an agreement that each has found to be mutually beneficial. It is a contracted business arrangement.

A Quixtar independent business owner is a partner. An IBO has joined in the work to make Quixtar.com the most successful Web site on the Internet. The IBO program has nothing to do with being sticky—and everything to do with being a member of a team, creating an alliance. I prefer to think of it as Quixtar's "Alliance Factor." It is that element of creating lasting partnerships with loyal online shoppers that will propel Quixtar.com to the heights of ecommerce success.

18. Extraordinary Value

The name of the game in ecommerce is value. It's not enough anymore to put an item up for sale and boast about your low, low price. Bill Gates has written: "There's no doubt that the

Internet is raising customer expectations," and he warns, "the middleman must add value."

In *Webonomics,* ecommerce journalist Evan Schwartz advised: "Building a long-term business on the Web is done not just by momentarily grabbing people's attention, but also by sustaining it with something of unique value." People want more; they expect more. And the Internet is giving it to them.

Quixtar.com opens up a whole new appreciation for what value is in the Digital Age. Acclaimed Quixtar leader and former professional athlete Tim Foley explained it to me like this: "We have a totally different understanding of what value is. Value is about real convenience; it's about unique, quality products that improve your life; it's about familiar, proven brand names and the best customer service. And value is about building solid, dependable relationships between people. But value is mostly about providing an opportunity for you to benefit yourself and your family. The ultimate value with Quixtar is that you can use it to create wealth for you and your family and achieve whatever dreams you may have in life."

The extraordinary value at Quixtar.com is that you can use that one-of-a-kind, online service to power a business of your very own that has the potential to make you quite wealthy. The last time I checked, neither Yahoo, Amazon.com, nor AOL offered anything remotely similar.

19. Open Door Opportunity

Perhaps one of the most obvious reasons that Quixtar.com spells success is the fact that its founders have created one of the most promising, accessible opportunities of the Digital Age. Quixtar's IBO option gives each of us a chance to reap the rewards of the Internet Revolution—regardless of race, gender, class, religious affiliation, marital status, job experience, you name it.

You do not have to pass a series of interviews with high-level Quixtar executives to start taking advantage of the opportunity. You do not have to take any tests, prepare a detailed resume, audition, or prove yourself to anyone. You simply must have a reason to succeed and a willingness to learn—and be ready to work.

"With Quixtar," Andy Andrews observed, "you're not just a faceless customer on the Web, you're a partner. You're an independent business owner, and your success is Quixtar's success. We're all working together. It's your store, your Web site. You get a piece of everything you buy. You get a piece of everything you refer."

Ken Harris is a partner with Cannondale Associates, a cutting-edge marketing and sales consulting firm: "People have been watching the Internet and have seen all these nanosecond millionaires who are created from start-up companies, and they feel like they haven't been able to play. It's been like a closed game that they haven't been able to participate in. It's almost like you have to be either a twenty-something techie in Silicon Valley or a millionaire venture capitalist to get in on the game. But Quixtar changes all of that. Now Quixtar will start creating its own nanosecond millionaires.

"Quixtar broadens the horizons," Harris continued. "It allows other people—everyman and everywoman—to really participate in this huge movement. It makes it possible for people to use the very latest technologies to get a little closer to their dreams. From that point of view, I think that the Quixtar model is much more friendly than a lot of the other Internet strategies out there. I have no doubt that Quixtar.com will be one of the premiere, successful ecommerce sites on the Web. And internationally, I think it has a lot of potential as well."

I asked Paul Miller, president of the Independent Business Owners Association Board and one of the principal business leaders who helped create Quixtar.com, what he thought was the most critical factor that would contribute to Quixtar's success. His answer hit on this very theme: that the IBO opportunity gives anyone the chance to play a key role in this momentous, historic event.

"I think that is the most exciting thing about Quixtar," he told me. "We're all players now. Instead of sitting up in the bleachers and watching other people become successful with the Internet, all of a sudden we're down on the field making it happen. And the best part of it is that anyone can join us. Anyone who wants to be a leader and benefit from this technological revolution can be a player now."

20. It Works

The last reason I believe Quixtar.com is achieving great success with its high-tech, high-touch business model is simple: It works. The opportunity to build wealth through ecommerce–based affiliate referrals and changing buying habits is very real. Quixtar's IBO option is one of the most significant opportunities of the new millennium.

"I'm absolutely wowed by what they've put together," David Rush of Kurt Salmon Associates concluded. "I think the concept is incredible, and I have to believe their ability to execute it, given the experience of their business leaders, will be very good. It's a fantastic step in the right direction, and something I think a lot of companies will pay attention to."

Quixtar leader and speaker Bo Short advised: "Let's not become so enamored with the sophistication of this new business model or with the technology that we forget that at its core is one of the greatest opportunities existing today. My wife, Sandy, and I never saw this opportunity as a means to an end, but literally as a means to a beginning. Each and every one of us has dreams in our life, things we want to accomplish, things we want to look back at one day and say we did. I see owning your own business powered by Quixtar as a way to do those things."

THE SYNERGY OF high-touch marketing combined with the boom in online shopping, plus each of the twenty distinct reasons we have looked at, all come together to make Quixtar.com one of the most successful ventures of the new Internet economy. That all these advantages could be integrated into one business model is truly revolutionary. Quixtar represents a quantum leap in marketing. First there was direct sales. Then came the World Wide Web and ecommerce. And now Quixtar.com.

Bo Short is a well-known author and entrepreneur. He has spoken in twenty countries around the globe to more than one million people. As president of the American Leadership Foundation he shares his experiences with Fortune 500 companies and high school and university students. Bo spent the early part of his career as a turn-around specialist, assisting ailing companies. He serves on the Advisory Board of KIDS, Inc., and the Boys and Girls Clubs of America Government Relations Committee. He and his wife, Sandy, are two of the most sought-after speakers and teachers of the Quixtar business.

Q. You've obviously had an impressive career in the traditional business world. Why Quixtar? In other words, what is it about Quixtar as a business opportunity that you find attractive?

A. "Primarily two things. First, when you look at the ownership and who's backing the venture, you can't help but be impressed. This is a value-based organization with the utmost integrity. Any entrepreneur worth his or her salt wants to build something that will last. You look to build a business on a solid foundation. In their history in business, the DeVos and Van Andel families have demonstrated that they have that integrity, that solid foundation. They've shown that to be the case many times over. You know that when they get behind something, it's not only going to do well, it's going to last.

"The business leaders who have affiliated with them over the years share those values. They demonstrate the same integrity, progressiveness, and long-term thinking. I feel comfortable as a business person knowing that my time, my energy, and my own capital will be invested wisely when I partner with these people.

"Second, each person working with this model as an independent business owner has something to gain and something to lose. Everybody connected together in this web has something at stake. You're not just working a job here. Your success or failure depends on your efforts. That way, everyone has the potential of winning or losing. And when that is the case, then people don't approach this opportunity with a job-with-a-wage mentality. That's not what this is about.

"When people are involved with something where the alternatives are success or failure, it compels them to think differently about their efforts. They start to think like entrepreneurs. We've created an environment and a business model that helps bring out the entrepreneur in each and every person we work with."

Q. And what exactly is that entrepreneurial thinking you refer to?

A. "It means organizing your thoughts and actions around these five basic principles: vision, courage, perseverance, responsibility, and character. When I founded the American Leadership Foundation, I'd interviewed a lot of successful people from a variety of different endeavors—sports, the arts, politics, business. Throughout those conversations, they all emphasized these same principles. Success in anything, not just in business with the Quixtar model but in anything at all, will depend on how well you can cultivate your own entrepreneurial thinking and develop those five principles in all that you do."

Q. Let me ask you this question, and please feel free to speak candidly: Aren't there a lot of people who just won't make it? I mean, isn't it only a small percentage of Quixtar IBOs who will create great wealth?

A. "Yes. But that is nothing unique to the Quixtar opportunity. Think about it, only a small percentage of people make it in most anything. Like learning to play the piano, only a small percentage of all the people who start taking lessons ever stick to it long enough to learn to play well. This opportunity is like anything else that requires practice and commitment. So if only the minority of people make large incomes, you have the opportunity now to be in the minority. Only those who are willing to invest the time and energy it takes will build successful businesses. It's not based on what your boss thinks about you, or who you know, or how many degrees are on your wall. It's all based on your willingness to put forth the effort to make it. It's a proven formula: those who do will create great wealth."

Q. Look at the attributes that it takes to become a successful Quixtar leader. If you had to pick just one that you believe is most important, what would it be?

A. "Without hesitation, I'd say the ability to persevere. The one big thing that blows most people out of the water in anything, not just this business model, is their inability to keep going. They quit. They don't learn how to manage their own frustration, and they stop—oftentimes right before they would have reached success. And again, this is nothing unique to the Quixtar IBO opportunity. This is true in everything we do. Most people want certain things, but they are not willing to continually work toward achieving them, especially when they hit roadblocks.

"All the people I've ever met who have achieved any level of success in their lives always have the same story: they failed, they failed, they failed, they failed, and then they made it. Do you see? They just never gave up trying. If I had to pick one thing, I'd say that was the most important key to success. It's like Napoleon said: The greatest attribute of a solider is not loyalty, it's not courage, it's endurance."

Q. One of the great lessons that Quixtar teaches the rest of the business world is the fine-tuned ability to build teams of entrepreneurs.

A. "I've never seen anything like it anywhere in corporate America. It's something they all aspire to. I can't tell you how many top executives I've talked with who would love to flatten out their organizations and build real teams. It's just a better way of doing business. But they're all too committed to the 'boss-manager-employee' paradigm. With Quixtar, there are no bosses in the picture. There are leaders who have more knowledge and experience. But they are not your bosses. You are your own boss. And you are your own employee. And if you're willing to be the toughest boss you've ever had, you're going to be one of the most successful people you've ever known."

> **Y**ou know it's a good deal. It's cutting edge. It's the future. This is it. Don't spend your life looking back, saying, "I should have done that."

Q. Anything you would like people to keep in mind as they encounter the Quixtar IBO opportunity?

A. "I think one of the biggest challenges people face is that they see something that they know in their gut is a good deal, but they walk right by it. And then five, ten, or fifteen years later they say, 'I could have done that.' With the Quixtar IBO option, you know it's a good deal. It's cutting edge. It's the future. This is it. Don't spend your life looking back, saying, 'I should have done that.' I read a great quote the other day: Write while there's ink in the pen. In other words, invest yourself now. When successful people see a good deal, they pursue it. They don't sit back and wait to watch and see what everyone else does. This is one of the greatest adventures you'll ever experience. It's the future calling you."

Q. Any final thoughts?

A. "Let's not become so enamored with the sophistication of this new business model or with the technology that we forget that at its core is one of the greatest opportunities existing today. Sandy and I never saw this opportunity as a means to an end but literally as a means to a beginning. Each and every one of us has dreams in our life, things we want to accomplish, things we want to look back one day and say we did. I see owning your own business powered by Quixtar as a way to do those things. My greatest success in life is that I'm the kind of husband I've always wanted to be. And I'm the kind of dad I've always wanted to be. That's because this opportunity has given me the freedom and the time to be with my family and not have to spend all day in a stressful job. Life's too short."

Bill Florence was one of the key leaders on the team of business owners that helped to create Quixtar.com. As co-chair of the Growth Committee with Paul Miller and vice president of the Independent Business Owners Association Board, Bill was closely involved in every aspect of the project since the very beginning. Bill and his wife, Peggy, are two of the most noteworthy and admired leaders affiliated with Quixtar today.

Q. Bill, you were involved with the traditional business model for many years. So you have seen things evolve and change over time. And you were right there helping to make Quixtar happen. What are your thoughts on this transformation, here at the dawn of the millennium?

A. "With the Growth Committee we wanted to aim the business where the world was going, not where the world is now. We wanted to shoot out into the future. As I see it, the mainstream has finally moved into the market that we've been in for forty years. The motto of the old traditional business we worked with was 'Shop Without Going Shopping.' We've pioneered the whole concept of in-home shopping for decades. And now everyone is trying to do what we figured out how to do a long time ago. We've already got the warehouses, the delivery system, the customer service, the ordering process, the whole infrastructure in place to handle this. All the new companies on the Web are struggling to catch up and build the infrastructure they need. But we've already got it all in place.

"Plus, we've got the high-touch teams and leaders out there who know how to put all that technology to use. There is tremendous cohesiveness in what we do. We've got a million people across North America who aren't just Quixtar consumers. They're entrepreneurs. They're our partners. These are people we see and work with all the time. And their success is our success. Even if Bill Gates went out to recruit and train the teams that we already have in place, it would cost him billions upon billions of dollars. And there's no telling how many years it would take him to do it. Quixtar isn't just the best about the past. It's what's best about the future, too. We are the marketing organization of the twenty-first century: people joined together all across the world. We're making history together."

Q. That really is one of the most impressive things about Quixtar: the fact that you build these extensive teams of business owners, one relationship at a time. And you do it off-line, not in a chat room on the Web.

A. "This business won't be built in cyber-space. We're taking advantage of cyber-space to make everything easier, to get rid of time-consuming paperwork and the distribution of products. There has never been a home-based business like the ones powered by Quixtar, not even close. But the business will be built with high-touch, by getting out where people actually live and work. This isn't about people alone in their homes on the computer. This is about looking people in the eye, shaking hands, working side by side. It's that blend of high-tech and high-touch that makes us the model for the future.

"People need help with all this stuff. Ask all the people who've learned to turn on a computer and get on the Internet: chances are someone sat there with them and showed them how to do it. Someone was there to answer their questions and show them the way. I think that's a big part about what we are do-

> Just concentrate on helping other people, and the wealth will come. I've seen it happen many, many times. Work for someone else's success, and this business will work for you.

ing. People are out there right now teaching and leading and showing people the way. They're helping people do things they didn't know they could do. The more that these new technologies become a part of our lives, the more people will to need someone there to take the time and help them learn. That's the most rewarding thing about what we're doing: seeing people realize that they can do it, that they are capable. I can't tell you how great it is to watch someone succeed whom you've helped get there. It's the best thing about what we do."

Q. And helping someone succeed doesn't happen without some effort.

A. "Right. Keep in mind that this is a business. The technology is phenomenal, the very best. And we're taking every advantage we can of the Internet. But if you don't work the business, it's not going to work for you. The compensation plan we have in place can't be beat by any other company. That's a fact.

"If people work hard, they're going to make a lot of money. Along those same lines, if they don't work hard, they're not going to make anything. That's how the IBO business model works. This business is an opportunity. It's not a lottery ticket. You will have to put forth the effort and work out a plan of action. Just concentrate on helping other people, and the wealth will come. I've seen it happen many, many times. Work for someone else's success, and this business will work for you."

Q. It must be a real joy for you and all the Quixtar leaders to watch this project take off as it has. You've created the most successful new business model of the twenty-first century.

A. "Everybody deserves a lot of credit. The DeVos and Van Andel families made sure from the very start that this was first class. They brought in the best technical partners we could have with Microsoft and Fry Multimedia, t-dah! and Vignette. They spared no expense. Whatever it took to make it the best, they said okay. Ken McDonald and his team have been right on top of this project from day one—people like John Parker,

Claire Zevalkink, and Randy Bancino. They've all worked around the clock and have been totally focused on making Quixtar a success. The leaders in all the organizations, everybody on the Growth Committee, and the Board has done a great job.

"And ,of course, none of it would have happened if it had not been for Dexter Yager and Bill Britt, who put the Growth Committee together in the first place. They have been committed to our success for over thirty years. And we wouldn't be here today to see Quixtar.com if not for all their hard work and efforts. Their leadership and their vision were critical every step along the way."

CHAPTER SEVEN

Into the New
Millennium

W E BEGAN THIS book by looking back to see what lessons the past could offer us about innovation and times of great change. We learned that the Internet Revolution is the beginning of a new era in human history. Hundreds of millions of people around the world are now using emerging technologies that were once limited to the labs of technical experts and computer engineers.

Amazing devices and inventions are fast becoming part of mainstream life. As a result, the ways that we live and work will be dramatically and irreversibly affected. From here on out, the rules have changed. It is an exciting time to be alive.

In this final chapter we'll look to the future—standing on the edge of the new millennium and peering out as far as we can see into the world that lies before us. But before we do, I want to tell you a "quick star" story.

My "Quick Star" Story

This story is true. It starts in Miss Johnson's fourth-grade class at Cardinal Forest Elementary School. It is "quiet" time—thirty minutes or so when all of us kids have to put our heads on our desks and take a rest.

On this day I have my head on the desk, and I am staring at the mobile of the solar system that hangs by the window across the room. You probably had something similar in one of your classrooms: an array of colored balls of various sizes suspended from a coat hanger that was supposed to represent the solar system. It has all nine planets—including the super big Jupiter and a tiny Mercury—the Earth's moon, and a big yellow ball for the Sun right in the middle.

There is a breeze coming in through the window, and the mobile of planets slowly turns back and forth. I remember finding that mobile so fascinating, like a 3-D map of the heavens. It made everything so compact and orderly.

The day she brought the mobile to class, Miss Johnson told us kids all the names of the planets. We laughed when she said Pluto—I mean, come on, we all know that's a dog's name. She also explained to us that the Sun is a giant ball of fire sitting in space—which the planets circle around in their orbits. When she told us that the stars in the night sky were actually faraway suns, well, if it is possible for a fourth-grader to have his mind blown, that certainly did it for me.

IT IS NOW about seven years later. I'm sitting in physics class in high school, and I'm bored. I have my head on my desk, watching the teacher walk back and forth in front of the room. He's talking about the solar system—something about a million miles and zillion light years—but I'm not paying all that much attention.

By this time, that fourth-grade classroom mobile of the planets and Sun has become totally fixed in my mind. Whenever I imagine the solar system, I instantly conjure up a mental image of those nine colorful balls all lined up, circling around a yellow Sun suspended from a coat hanger. That is my model for the solar system. It is the tidy mental picture that I have grown up with. I am very comfortable with it. But my physics teacher is about to change all of that.

He pauses for a moment, perhaps aware that mine is not the only sleepy face staring back at him. Then he walks silently to the back of the room, disappears into a storage closet, and comes walking out carrying a bowling ball. He doesn't say a word. I'm awake now. The whole class is awake now. We pivot in our seats and watch him as he walks back to the front of the room. He sets the bowling ball on his desk with a thud, turns to us, and says: "To picture how big the solar system really is, I want you to imagine that the Sun is the size of this bowling ball." Okay, I can do that. The Sun is the size of a bowling ball.

He then reaches into his desk and pulls out an opened bag of sunflower seeds. He pours some into his hand and eats them. Then he digs out another seed and holds it up to the class: "See this little sunflower seed?" I lean forward in my chair. "Picture a little round sunflower seed. This is about how big the Earth would be if the Sun were the size of a bowling ball." He then walks to the back of the room and disappears again into the storage closet, where we hear him yell: "And this is about how far away the Earth would be from the Sun."

Then he strolls back into the classroom, chewing on the "Earth" sunflower seed. "And do you know where Pluto would be?" he asks, leaning against his desk. There is a quiet hush. "If the Sun were the size of that bowling ball, the Earth would be a round sunflower seed all the way back there in the closet, and Pluto would be about the size of a pin-head half a mile away."

As a business, Quixtar represents a system of cooperative action where every individual is on a path moving forward. Every action taken is a step in the direction of an ultimate goal.

At that moment the bell rings and my classmates bolt from their seats. My teacher grins and folds his arms in front of him. I sit motionless. What happened to the colored balls hanging in a neat row on a coat hanger? Suddenly, that little fourth-grade mobile seems like a toy. Suddenly, space is unbelievably endless. My mind is blown again.

THE LAST SCENE of my true "quick star" story takes place three years after that. I am a college sophomore sitting in the library, pretending to study. My friend next to me is cramming for an astronomy test, with a book open in front of him.

I lean over and look at some of the pictures in my friend's book. One is a sketch of the Sun, drawn to look like it is shooting through space, with the planets spiraling around it as it goes. "What's that?" I ask. He calmly looks at me and says: "That's what our solar system looks like. The Sun is moving through space at about twelve miles a second."

That can't be, I think to myself. In my mind's eye, the Sun is like a big, fiery bowling ball sitting in space surrounded by distant sunflower seeds and pin heads. "I thought the Sun sits in space and the planets orbit around it," I tell my friend.

"The planets do revolve around the sun," he explains, "but the Sun doesn't just sit there. It's moving, too. And the planets orbit the Sun as it goes. Everything in space is moving."

"The Sun is *shooting through space*, really?" I am dumbfounded. This is news to me.

"Yeah, at over twelve miles a second."

"I had no idea," I say slowly. Then my friend laughs and says: "Yep, that's one quick star."

THIS STORY HAS come to my mind more than once while writing this book—at first because of the obvious "quick star" coincidence. But the more I thought about Quixtar.com, the more I began to see another meaning in this story.

It won't be news to some of you that the Sun is actually shooting through space—especially if you took a lot of science classes in school. But I didn't, and I'll never forget the moment I learned that fact. My whole model of the universe changed, just as it had in my physics class in high school.

As comforting and simple as I found that mobile hanging in my fourth-grade classroom, that's just not the way I think of the solar system now. Ever since that conversation in the college library, I have had a different model in mind: one in which the Sun is flying through space as the planets and their moons corkscrew around it. I call it the "quick star" model of the universe.

The Quixtar Model

When you think about it, Quixtar.com has a lot in common with my "quick star" model of the universe. As a business, Quixtar represents a system of cooperative action where every individual is on a path moving forward. Every action taken is a step in the direction of an ultimate goal. Like my "quick star" model of the universe, there is a rhythm and a synergy to Quixtar—everything clicks together in relationship to everything else. On one level, people are just doing their own thing, following their own paths. But from a larger perspective, they are all elements unified into one system, part of a team.

In the old model of the universe I imagined, the Sun sat like a heavy bowling ball in its spot in space as the planets went endlessly around it—around and around, never really going anywhere, always coming back to the same spot. That reminds me of the conventional home-to-work-to-home existence, where many people go around in circles their whole lives, never really feeling like they're making any progress or getting anywhere. But in a business powered by Quixtar, they become part of a system that is shooting ahead. It's a model of progress, of accomplishment, of moving forward into the future. It may not be twelve miles a second—but how does "nanosecond millionaire" sound?

THERE IS ANOTHER reason I told you my "quick star" story. I believe that Quixtar.com is the new model of business for the twenty-first century. Just as my own model of space changed as I grew older and learned new things, so, too, our model of business is changing as we learn new ways to integrate emerging technologies with commerce. Quixtar's high-tech, high-touch strategy represents the new way of doing business in the next millennium.

Remember what happened in the Industrial Revolution about two hundred years ago: Arkwright's factory system became the new model for business. Nearly everything about doing business changed. A vast network of cottage industries died out, replaced by mass production techniques. Formerly independent craftspeople became employees and began working long hours in factories. There were no laws passed that forced business owners to organize their ventures that way. It just happened. Entrepreneurs noticed that a business was more profitable the more they controlled workers, so this became the new model of success.

And recall what took place during the Corporate Revolution roughly one hundred years later: As new machines and technologies (like the typewriter, the telephone, and the adding machine) were introduced into the business environment, things changed again. A new standard model of business evolved: the corporation, which took control of the factory model and has dominated commerce ever since.

As children of the twentieth century, we all inherited this model. It was here before any of us, so we take it for granted. The corporate model of business is almost like part of the landscape. We are thus understandably curious, cautious, even suspicious of ways of doing business that don't follow the standard model we grew up with.

That is why people were so wary of franchises and the old referral-based marketing businesses when they first came on the scene—they were different, new, unconventional. But as you know, they worked.

All of which brings us to the Internet Revolution. With the flood of new technologies into society and the boom in electronic commerce, we are witnessing another shift from an old model to a new model. The century-old corporate structure will be transformed, reconfigured, and streamlined as it transitions to the Internet-based environment of the new millennium. What will the new model of business look like in the twenty-first century? I believe it will look like Quixtar.com.

What Makes Quixtar the Twenty-First-Century Model of Business?

WHEN I SAY that Quixtar is the model of business for the twenty-first century, I don't mean that Ford, Microsoft, and IBM will all necessarily have to develop affiliate-referral strategies and Tridigital marketing teams. But Quixtar has a number of important characteristics that any business hoping to make it in the new economy should heed. To that end, any company large or small that wants to prosper in the new millennium should take a close look at what makes Quixtar.com tick.

In their best-selling book *Net.gain,* authors John Hagel and Arthur G. Armstrong write that "bridging the gap between the way that traditional businesses are run" and the way that companies will have to operate with an Internet-based strategy "represents the single greatest challenge for senior management of existing companies. Most will need to adopt a mental model very different from the one they have in place."

To help them get started in forming a new mental model, here are a few key ingredients of the Quixtar formula that will characterize a successful business in the twenty-first century.

Get Connected—Remember the words of investment broker David Millican of Atlanta: "It's a dot com world. If you don't have a strategy that involves the Internet in some way, then you're kidding yourself." That is the first lesson that Quixtar.com offers the world of business: Go high-tech, and do it now.

Putting a dot com after the name of your company, however, should not be an end in itself. That's just the first step. The Internet should be part of an aggressive strategy to streamline operations, to add value and convenience, to make your company more versatile and adaptable, and to create new alliances and partnerships—all of which are priorities for any business in the new millennium. This is what the DeVos and Van Andel families and their business leaders have done by adapting their old business model to the Internet.

The Corporation Is Out. The Individual Is In—In their examination of the new Internet-based economy, authors Thomas Malone and Robert Laubacher of MIT's Sloan School of Management write that the new fundamental unit of business "is not the corporation but the individual." It's not about people working to make that big company successful. It's about that big company making its people successful.

We are witnessing the death of the archetypal "company man" and "company woman" who sacrifice everything—including family time and personal freedom—to make the boss happy and the company profitable. Instead, companies will succeed in the twenty-first century by placing a priority value on the dreams and goals of those who work with them.

Well-known Quixtar leader Chuck Vogt describes it like this: "When I was working in corporate America, I never went to my job and had my boss sit me down and say, 'You know Chuck, our new focus for the year is your wife's car. We've noticed it's getting a little old, and it's time you all had a new one. So we're going to refocus all our efforts this year as a corporation and see if we can't help you.'

"And I never went to work and walked into a board meeting and they said, 'We're going to see if we can find a way to give Chuck more time with his family.' It never happened, not once. But with Quixtar's IBO program, that's the focus. Success is not based on working a set number of hours a week for a set amount of money, week after week, year after year. Success is based on achieving what you want to achieve and helping others to do the same."

Successful companies of the new millennium will follow the Quixtar example and personalize their relations: focusing on the goals of individuals and providing a platform of programs that will help them achieve their dreams.

The Ultimate Value: Opportunity—Winning businesses of the twenty-first century will find new ways to bring opportunity to those who work with them. In the new millennium opportunity means choice, flexibility, convenience, fairness, and freedom. It means fewer walls and more doors. It means the chance for unlimited achievement. Initiative, creativity, autonomy, and hard work will be rewarded above all. The more businesses integrate opportunity into all that they do, the more prosperous they will become.

Consider the opportunity of Quixtar's IBO program. "Quixtar broadens the horizons," Ken Harris of Cannondale Associates commented. "It allows other people—everyman and everywoman—to really participate in this huge movement. It makes it possible for people to use the very latest technologies to get a little closer to their dreams."

And as Quixtar leader Tim Foley said: "Value is mostly about providing an opportunity, with the chance to benefit yourself and your family. The ultimate value with Quixtar is that you can use it to create wealth for you and your family and achieve whatever dreams you may have in life."

Have you ever stopped to wonder why people are flocking to the Internet? It's not because they especially enjoy sitting in front of computer screens or waiting for Web pages to download. It's because the Internet represents *opportunity*. It represents the chance to learn, to discover, to have fun, to move forward in their lives.

"People are coming to the Web in droves," Quixtar entrepreneur Jody Victor said. "They're fascinated by it. They want convenience. They see it as a way to improve their lives, to take control. They're tired of people telling them how it's going to be and what they can and can't do in their lives. People are just sick and tired of the limited options. They're coming to the Web to find opportunities that don't exist anywhere else—new options, new business models, new futures."

In their examination of the new Internet-based economy, authors Thomas Malone and Robert Laubacher of MIT's Sloan School of Management write that the new fundamental unit of business "is not the corporation but the individual." It's not about people working to make that big company successful. It's about that big company making its people successful.

In the old corporate model, business provided jobs and paid people according to what that position was worth to the company. In the new Quixtar world, companies provide opportunity and incentive, are willing to share the wealth, and reward those who do the work. They encourage entrepreneurial, achievement-oriented thinking—not the wage-driven, job mentality of the past.

"Even within corporations," *Fortune* magazine reported in May, 1999, "there is a growing tendency to rely on individual initiative, on independent profit centers free to take risks and do it their way. Information technology ended up deconstructing instead of reinforcing the corporation."

"The new work environment," comments business theorist and author Michael Hammer, "expects everyone to be a kind of entrepreneur: self-starting, autonomous, responsible," where a career path is "based not on hierarchical advancement but on personal development."

Business leader Bo Short explained how this approach is put to use with Quixtar: "Each person working with this model as an independent business owner has something to gain and something to lose. Everybody connected together in this web has something at stake. You're not just working a job here. Your success or failure depends on your efforts. That way, everyone has the potential of winning or losing. And when that is the case, then people don't approach this opportunity with a job-with-a-wage mentality. That's not what this is about.

"When people are involved with something where the alternatives are success or failure, it compels them to think differently about their efforts. They start to think like entrepreneurs. We've created an environment and a business model that helps bring out the entrepreneur in each and every person we work with."

As we move into the twenty-first century, the more that companies are willing to offer opportunity and cultivate entrepreneurial thinking, the more successful they will become.

Create Community—Since it's no longer about the corporation but about the individual, people connecting to people is more important to business now than it has ever been. The Quixtar approach is the leading example of a successful high-touch strategy that creates community.

Business in the twenty-first century is not about people coming together in impersonal, conventional workplaces for a predetermined number of hours, five days a week. It's about people coming together online for special events and offline in living rooms, meeting rooms, and convention halls. It's all about personal relationships, people skills, and individual action. Remember the words of Evan Schwartz from his book *Webonomics:* "The Web is not a mass medium. It's a niche medium, a personal medium, and an interactive medium."

In his book *The Caring Economy,* Internet strategist and entrepreneur Gerry McGovern describes the Digital Age as a time when "technology will become transparent and people will become paramount. If businesses want long-term success in the Digital Age, they need to care about people and about the issues that are important to people." McGovern declares that "community and commerce are inherently intertwined—you cannot have one without the other."

Companies that endeavor to follow Quixtar's lead and create community, both within and among organizations, will do very well in the new economy.

Alliances and Partnerships—One of the most important characteristics of a successful business in the twenty-first century is its ability to create productive alliances, on a continuing basis at many levels. Connectivity, networks, communication, linking, access, cooperation—these are the forms and functions of the World Wide Web. Success in ecommerce will depend on how well companies maximize their Alliance Factor and synthesize the nature of the Web into the dynamics of their business.

Businesses in the new millennium will do well to reevaluate their relationships between customers and employees—going so far as to question the very merit of the terms. Following the Quixtar.com example, the preferred approach will be to empower customers by creating long-term alliances with them: as *independent partners.* Alliances encourage autonomy and initiative, while leveraging time and effort.

A tremendous value is placed on team-building in the Quixtar model of business: Your *partner's* success is *your* success. Because of the nature of the alliance, you achieve your goals by helping other people achieve theirs. In the Digital Age of globalization, this strategy will be critical—for companies, governments, communities, and for individuals.

"In the Quixtar model," entrepreneur Brian Hays explained, "you don't win the game alone, it's a team effort. And the incentives are there for us to help each other, encourage one another, and help one another achieve our goals. That's how it all works."

Value-Based Strategies—Another component of the Quixtar model of business that will be an essential element of any successful company in the twenty-first century is value-based leadership and decision-making. In the Digital Age, doing the right thing has become a good business move.

Quixtar leader Fred Harteis described the success of Quixtar.com as being "built on solid principles to protect the individual. The more integrity you put in, the better your business will perform. This business doesn't work with hype, games, or taking advantage of someone. So your first priority is to give of yourself. It's an old formula. But in our business, it's a formula that can make you wealthy."

Paul Miller, president of the Board of Quixtar's Independent Business Owners Association, agreed: "That's the part that most people who aren't involved with this business have a hard time understanding. People just aren't used to seeing a business leader go on and on about caring for others, and serving other people. That's just not something you hear too much about in the regular business world. When some people first hear it, it makes them wonder if this is even a real business.

"But we're different. That's how our business works. We've got a business model where the more you give, the more you care, the more you work to make other people successful, the more success you will have. I'll tell you this much: The only way you will create wealth in a business powered by Quixtar is to be a man or woman of integrity, plain and simple. We value honesty, we value family, and we value long-term thinking. And we value them not just because it's the right thing to do, but because that's how you become successful with our business model. Yes, there is the potential for incredible wealth with our compensation plan. But success in your own business, fueled by all the advantages that Quixtar offers, will bring you so much more than money."

The New Efficiency—Disintermediation (getting rid of the middleman) will be one of the keys to a totally new efficiency in the twenty-first century. For example, efficient shopping no longer means creating wider aisles, clearly marked specials, or more checkout lines. It means eliminating the trip to the store altogether and having products delivered to people's homes. As is the case with the Quixtar.com model, getting rid of conventional middlemen in as many transactions as possible will be the first important step toward creating a new model of efficiency and service.

Disintermediation will not only occur *outside* of a company or organization but *within* it as well. Middle management and those executives who simply supervise the actions of others will have little place in the new way of doing things.

Michael Hammer, a leading business theorist and the author of *Beyond Reengineering*, has written: "The classic industrial model in which workers perform specialized tasks under layers of managerial oversight is completely unsuited to the new economic environment. It is too slow, too costly, too inflexible to satisfy powerful customers. The result has been nothing less than the abandonment of that model."

Hammer continues: "Customers will not accept the errors and excess costs that result when work is handed off from one narrow taskworker to another, so jobs are becoming much bigger and broader. Customers will not abide the delays that ensue when workers must bring all decisions to managers, so responsibility is being devolved to people on the front lines.

Customers will not tolerate the inflexibility and complexity that come from dealing with a host of departments, from sales to service to production to accounting, so the walls between these departments have been knocked down and work is increasingly being done by teams of people from different departments. Customers will not be satisfied with yesterday's products, so innovation has become the new routine and learning is a fundamental part of everyone's job. These changes are not confined to a few companies; they are taking place across all sectors of the economy."

The Pyramid Is Out. The Web Is In—The successful businesses of the twenty-first century will adopt the Web as the model for organization, replacing the old corporate-pyramid structure. A networked business model, as exemplified by the independent business owners affiliated with Quixtar.com, is decentralized and promotes self-reliance and team-centered cooperation.

Business analysts Malone and Laubacher have observed: "With the introduction of powerful personal computers and broad electronic networks—the coordination technologies of the twenty-first century—the economic equation changes. Because information can be shared instantly and inexpensively among many people in many locations, the value of centralized decision making and expensive bureaucracies decreases. Individuals can manage themselves, coordinating their efforts through electronic links with other independent parties. Small becomes good.

"In one sense, the new coordination technologies enable us to return to the preindustrial organization model of tiny, autonomous businesses—businesses of one or of a few—

conducting transactions with one another in a market. But there's one crucial difference: Electronic networks enable these microbusinesses to tap into the global reservoirs of information, expertise, and financing that used to be available only to large companies. The small companies enjoy many of the benefits of the big without sacrificing the leanness, flexibility, and creativity of the small."

Winning businesses of the twenty-first century will find new ways to bring opportunity to those who work with them. In the new millennium opportunity means choice, flexibility, convenience, fairness, and freedom. It means fewer walls and more doors. It means the chance for unlimited achievement. Initiative, creativity, autonomy, and hard work will be rewarded above all.

The authors conclude that the best way to understand successful organizations of the twenty-first century is "not as traditional hierarchies, but as confederations of entrepreneurs, united only by a common brand name."

One principal advantage of the web-structured organization is its flexibility. For example, no longer will workers have to gather in one central location for the business to function. Columnist Susan Paynter, who often writes about the issues facing working parents, wrote in *Working Mother* magazine: "Much of the next century's work will be decentralized, done at home or in satellite offices on a schedule tailored to fit workers' lives and the needs of their families. Nonetheless, being part of a virtual community will never entirely replace the need for in-person connections right here at home. That's why workers of the future will also flock to satellite work centers in their neighborhoods. Many will have amenities—provided by companies or entrepreneurs—that bring people together, as they used to gather around the watercooler."

"At the heart of all these changes," Paynter determines, "is the fact that we have finally begun to separate the idea of work from the place where we do it. And that will make blending work and family a lot easier for many people."

With its networks of affiliated, independent businesses—most of which are individuals or family groups working from their homes—Quixtar is leading the way by bringing this new model to ecommerce.

Mentors, not Managers—The workplace manager is an outdated remnant of a business model that is over two hundred years old. Created for the textile mills in the Industrial Revolution, the role of the manager was to watch over employees and control their actions. Now autonomy and empowerment—not control and domination—are the hallmarks of a progressive company. As demonstrated by the Quixtar model, managers have no place in the business of the twenty-first century. Instead, mentors lead the owners of affiliated businesses through a program of ongoing education and personal development.

As Quixtar entrepreneur Bo Short explained, mentoring is more than simply providing an example for someone to follow: "As a leader, you start teaching perseverance, courage, vision, character, and responsibility by demonstrating those principles in action—by providing an example. But you have to go beyond that. There are plenty of great examples out there. We have to meet people halfway and show them how to do it. The goal is not simply to be a good example but to be a mentor.

"With Quixtar," he continued, "there are no bosses in the picture. There are leaders who have more knowledge and experience. But they are not your bosses. You are your own boss. And you are your own employee. And if you're willing to be the toughest boss you've ever had, you're going to be one of the most successful people you've ever known."

Quixtar leader Chuck Vogt agreed that the mentoring program is absolutely critical: "Hal and Susan Gooch are on the team of leaders that heads up our organization. Hal said something the other day that I will never forget. He said, 'People seldom improve when their mentors are themselves.' I thought that was so powerful. When I was in the corporate world, there was someone in front of me in the corporation who had been there a few years longer than me. But he was really looking out for himself. That's how the business worked. There was no mentor program, because if he helped me too much, then I just might get his job one day.

"But when you look at the Quixtar model, we encourage and develop mentorships all along the way. Part of our job is to get people to really give some thought to what they want to achieve in life. I think a lot of people out there today just don't know what they want. They've spent most of their lives with someone else telling them what to do. So when it comes to their own dreams and goals, they just don't know. A lot of people haven't even thought about it all that much. That's where we start as leaders: helping people think clearly about what *they* want out of life, not what their bosses want out of them."

GO HIGH-TECH NOW, focus on the individual, offer real opportunity, create community, build alliances, and get a value-based strategy. Think "new efficiency"; web, not pyramid; and

mentors, not managers—these are some of the characteristics of successful companies of the twenty-first century. And
they each describe a critical element of Quixtar.com.

The DeVos and Van Andel families and their business leaders who put Quixtar together did not invent these principles.
But they did weave them into one unified whole and have
demonstrated to the world how effectively the principles can
be put to use in the new economy. Instead of merely reinventing an old model for a new medium, they created something
strikingly original—an archetype for the future. That a company comes to the Internet with all these progressive qualities
seamlessly intertwined, enjoying all the superior advantages we
discussed before, is indeed historic and revolutionary.

This Quixtar revolution represents a turning point in
ecommerce—a new chapter in the story of the Digital Age.
The Quixtar approach is the model of business that companies will emulate in one form or another for years to come.
The success of Quixtar.com and the achievements of every
affiliated independent business owner will stand as a testament to the power of a high-tech, high-touch business strategy
in the twenty-first century.

HAL AND SUSAN Gooch are internationally acclaimed
Quixtar leaders and teachers. Just a few days before Quixtar.com
officially opened its virtual doors to the world, Hal shared some
of his thoughts with me about the Quixtar future.

"We've been fortunate to have worked with the DeVos
and Van Andel families and all the other business leaders for
many years," he said. "The experiences we've had and the
friends we've made, these have been blessings to Susan and
me. But one of the greatest things of all is to be able to be a

part of the team that is launching Quixtar. One day we will be able to say that we were there on September 1, 1999, when Quixtar went online. This is history. This is a new era. The door is opening to the twenty-first century, and Quixtar is right there ready to go.

"This is a time of incredible change," he continued. "Computers and the Internet are changing the way that we do business. And Quixtar is at the forefront, showing the rest of the world what is possible. Companies will look at Quixtar as an example to follow. They'll wonder how we did it—how did we manage to create the biggest ecommerce site on the Internet so fast? How did we bring in all the partners and pull all the people together to make this happen? And how do we make it work so well? All eyes will be on us. We're the organization, the Web site, and the opportunity that others will look up to."

THE INTERNET REVOLUTION is ushering in an era of new opportunities and new models. It's a time for each of us to reevaluate our plans and our goals. Where are you headed? How do you plan to get there? Are you going around in circles? Or are you racing ahead to some greater destination?

Quixtar.com provides a new way for us to think about what a company is really capable of. It raises the bar in ecommerce, providing a new benchmark for what it means to create community; to offer convenience, service, options—and most of all, opportunity. Quixtar is also a new way of thinking about what we as individuals are capable of. Possibilities abound.

THE TECHNOLOGY THAT makes this new era possible is truly remarkable. And it becomes ever more so each day. Computers become faster and easier to use. The Internet becomes more versatile, personable, and convenient. Wireless, handheld devices promise to open exciting new doors. So much of what was once science-fiction fantasy is fast becoming our reality. What will these wonders be capable of ten years from now? twenty years? fifty?

It's difficult to know specifically how these technologies will play out in the future. Every new advance introduces new avenues of research and unplanned possibilities. But I think there is a way for us to appreciate just how much things might change. So, grab your bike and let's go.

What the Bicycle Tells Us About the Future

YOU WANT TO take a glimpse at the future of high technology, computers, and the Internet? Then look at bicycles. You heard right, bicycles. They have more to tell us than you might at first think. First, a little background.

The modern-day bicycle had its origins in the late 1700s in France—although it didn't look much at all like the bicycles of today. It was described as a "wooden horse." There were no pedals, and you couldn't even steer the front wheel. You had to pick the thing up and point it in the direction you wanted to go, as you pushed along the ground with your feet.

In 1839 a Scottish blacksmith made improvements to the old model and created what would be more familiar to us today: it had a seat, pedals, two wheels, and could even be steered. But at 57 pounds with iron wheels, it wasn't very easy to ride.

In the early 1860s a Parisian coach builder invented what most people consider to be the first "modern bicycle." With pedals connected by a crankshaft to the front and rear wheels, it was much easier to use. The inventor managed to sell over 140 of the new cycles in the first year of production. Improvements and innovations soon followed, including wire-spoked wheels, solid rubber tires, and multiple gears. Some inventors even introduced steam-powered bicycles.

In 1877 Augustus Pope of Hartford, Connecticut, opened the first bicycle factory in the United States. Pope's claim to fame was his Columbia model bicycle, with its giant front wheel that you've probably seen in pictures. The Columbia was the bicycle of choice for many years, even though many found it hard to get on to and rather dangerous to ride.

> **D**isintermediation (getting rid of the middleman) will be one of the keys to a totally new efficiency in the twenty-first century. For example, efficient shopping no longer means creating wider aisles, clearly marked specials, or more checkout lines. It means eliminating the trip to the store altogether and having products delivered to people's homes.

Finally in 1885, Englishman John Starley, a former sewing machine maker, introduced the "Rover Safety" bicycle. With two wheels of equal size and a chain-driven rear wheel, the "safety" bike was a big hit. The old model highwheelers, with their riders way up off the ground, looked down on the new safety bikes (literally) and even referred to their riders as lowly "crocodiles" and "beetles."

Even though it was a strange-looking, unfamiliar invention at first, the low-to-the-ground safety bike caught on. Safety bikes were easier to get on and off of, easier to handle, and, well, safer. If the bike happened to tip over, you wouldn't fall five or six feet to the ground. People scrambled to buy the new safety bikes, which sparked a bicycling boom in the 1890s. Gradually, the older model bikes with their massive front wheels became less and less popular. The safety bike took over as the mainstream standard and became the model for all the bicycles that would follow.

It took about one hundred years for the bicycle to evolve from a heavy "wooden horse" with no pedals and no way to steer it, to a giant front-wheel monster, to the standard safety bike of modern times.

NOW, LET'S TALK about where we are today with all these emerging new technologies. When it comes to computers, the Internet, and the World Wide Web, I don't think we've even reached the safety-bike phase yet. Do you follow me? As far as the technology is concerned, we're still rumbling along on those huge front-wheel bicycles.

Sure, things have come a long, long way since the days people picked moths off the vacuum tubes of the ENIAC computer or since the first wires of the ARPAnet were installed. But Augustus Pope's Columbia bike in the 1870s with its giant front wheel was a big advance over the old "wooden horse" bikes, too. Here at the dawn of the twenty-first century, I believe we are just getting started. The "safety bike era" of the Internet is yet to come.

The safety bike made cycling accessible to a large number of people for the first time. It wasn't at all like the high-wheeled monsters that preceded it. To the great majority of people, those big bikes were unattractive, intimidating, clumsy, and dangerous. And most of all, they were anything but user-friendly. Yet anybody could climb aboard a safety bike and take off. If you got scared, you could stop and put your feet out and touch the ground. The safety bike was easy and reassuring. It wasn't anything like the way bikes used to be. It was almost as if you weren't up on a bicycle at all, but rather just gliding along.

WHERE ARE WE headed with all this new computer technology? What might the "safety-bike phase" of the Internet look like? For one thing, it might have little to do with a computer. Whenever we think of the Internet these days, we naturally think of computers. After all, without computers you don't have an Internet. But that will change. Industry leaders agree that as technology develops, every appliance and gadget you can think of will be linked to the Internet: refrigerators, microwave ovens, household lights, the family car, even your bicycle. Thanks to WebTV, television sets are already able to hook up to the Net. As time goes on, more and more devices will all be networked together and will have the ability to "talk" to each other.

Just imagine what could one day be: Your refrigerator will scan its own contents, see that you are low on orange juice, and add a new carton to the grocery list, which it automatically orders each week. Your microwave will sense what you have put inside it and will set the time and power level itself. The bathroom mirror could become a personalized viewing screen and give you the morning news as you brush your teeth. Besides alerting you to traffic patterns as you drive, your car will know when it is time for some routine maintenance, then will check with your calendar before it automatically sets up an appointment with the mechanic.

Perhaps you're on vacation, relaxing on a remote beach hundreds of miles from home, worried that you might have left the stove on—just grab a hand-held device lying on the sand next to you and find out. While you're at it, you can turn on the lawn sprinkler and feed the cats.

"Not thinking of the Internet in terms of your computer is an important first step toward understanding what the future might be like," said Gene DeRose of Jupiter Communications. "It basically gets down to this: All that technology will become *invisible*. For example, you don't think of your television set as high technology, even though it basically is. You don't think of your watch as advanced technology either, or your phone. But at some point, they all were. Even electricity was science fiction at one point. But now it's all throughout your home. We've just grown accustomed to it.

"As the technology becomes more a part of our lives, the fact that it is advanced technology gradually recedes. We become more aware of the uses and the purpose of products than of the technology inside them. Computers and the Internet aren't at that point yet. They're still at a stage where we are aware of the technology, and it even intimidates people."

The "safety-bike phase" of computers and the Internet will have arrived when people aren't even aware of using those technologies. They will become so much a part of our lives that we will hardly be aware of their presence. It's likely we won't even have the distinction of being online or offline. And our grandchildren will look with wide-eyed wonder as we tell them about the awful sounds that modems made, how long it took some Web pages to download, and what it was like to use a mouse.

BEYOND THAT, THINK about what has happened to bicycles since the modern safety bike was invented in 1885. We now have tiny bikes for children, racing bikes, off-road bikes, beach bikes, bicycles built for two, stunt bikes, bikes you can fold up and carry with you—even little bicycles for trained parrots to ride in bird shows. And if you want, someone could actually custom-build a bicycle just for you. In other words, bicycles have evolved to fit any lifestyle, any person, anywhere.

The same will happen with computers and the Internet. The technology will not only become "invisible" (so user-friendly you aren't aware you're using it); it will also become completely personalized to fit any individual, any family, or any organization.

And just as safety bikes led to mopeds, scooters, and motorcycles, so, too, the technology of the Internet Revolution will one day produce innovations that we haven't yet even dreamed of. This is a thrilling time. We are on the threshold of a grand era in human history.

Attention, Dreamers

I WAS VERY fortunate to have talked about some of these ideas with Dexter Yager just two days before the launch of Quixtar. Dexter is a legend of American business. He has worked very closely with the DeVos and Van Andel families for many years and, along with Quixtar leader Bill Britt, helped form the Growth Committee that was instrumental in the making of Quixtar.com.

"I'm not a computer, high-tech kind of guy," Dexter admitted to me with a laugh. "But I have been paying attention to what's happening. When you go into a restaurant, someone prints your bill out on a computer. At a gas station, you pay at the pump on a computer without having to go inside the store. People go on the Internet to do their banking, to go shopping, to buy and sell their stocks. I don't have to know much about computers to know that the world is changing. New technology is becoming more a part of our lives every day. And we have to learn to use it.

The successful businesses of the twenty-first century will adopt the Web as the model for organization, replacing the old corporate-pyramid structure. A networked business model, as exemplified by the independent business owners affiliated with Quixtar.com, is decentralized and promotes self-reliance and team-centered cooperation.

"I know new technologies make some people nervous," he said. "That's okay. But remember that the technology you're comfortable with today was brand new at one time, too. Yesterday's modern technology is today's toaster. The great inventions of yesterday are just the things you use to cook with now, or they're how you get your news, or communicate, or even cut your grass. Over time, these things become part of our lives. Now we're watching the arrival of the Internet and computers. All that new technology will be mainstream one day. And I believe that Quixtar.com will be as mainstream one day as the telephone.

"The Internet and Quixtar will bring people options," he concluded, "which a lot of people don't have right now. Options give people the chance to start dreaming again and thinking about their future. And with the high-tech and the high-touch together in one package, Quixtar will give people a way to make those dreams come true."

DEXTER YAGER'S INSIGHTFUL comments reminded me of something I'd read during my research. When I hung up the phone, I leafed through a few books and soon found the excerpt I was looking for. Reflecting on the revolutionary effect of the World Wide Web computer program he created, physicist Tim Berners-Lee remarked:

"I think the main intention was to make the thing fly. When you're really attached to a dream of how things could be, then you pursue that dream and it's very, very satisfying to see it work. The fact that the World Wide Web did work, I find is just exciting for itself. Exciting that you can have an idea and it can take off and it can happen. It means that dreamers all over the world should take off and not stop."

Now, close this book. Take off. And do not stop.

FOLLOWING IS A list of the key leaders and contributors who helped make Quixtar.com a reality

Key Corporate Staff

Dick DeVos—President

Steve Van Andel—Chairman

Dave Van Andel—Sr. VP/Managing Director of the Americas and Europe

Doug DeVos—Sr. VP/Managing Director of Asia & Global Distributor Relations

Ken McDonald—Sr. VP/Managing Director of the North American Business Region

Robin Horder-Koop—Vice President of North American Business Region

John Parker—Director of Business Relations

Claire Zevalkink—Director of Marketing

Randy Bancino—Sr. Manager of Internet Business Group

Dave Bamborough—Manager of ANA Administration

Kelly Savage—Director of Customer Service & Systems

Jim Hunking—General Manager of Amway of Canada

The Growth Committee

Established by Bill Britt and Dexter Yager

Billy Florence, Co-Chairman

Paul Miller, Co-Chairman

Bob Andrews, Mark Crawford, Greg Duncan, Jim Floor, Tim Foley, Don Storms, and Jody Victor

Quixtar's Independent Business Owners Association Board 1999

The Officers: President Paul Miller, Vice President Billy Florence, Secretary/Treasurer Jody Victor

Executive Committee: Paul Miller, Billy Florence, Jody Victor, Don Storms, Scott Michael, Jim Dornan, Jerry Meadows, and Rex Renfrow

Working with the Executive Committee: Past President/ Moderator Bob Zeender

President Cabinet's Representatives: Bill Britt and Dexter Yager

Legal and Ethics Committee: Chairman, Jody Victor

Members: Billy Florence, Hal Gooch, Jack Daughery, Fred Harteis, Paul Miller, and Ron Hale

Awards and Recognition Committee: Chairman Randy Haugen

Members: Scott Michael, Mark Crawford, Brad Duncan, Louie Carrillo, Joe Foglio, and Bobby Howard

International Committee: Chairman Don Storms

Members: Rex Renfrow, Jim Elliott, Craig Bishop, Jim Dornan, Terry Felber, and Glenn Shoffler

Business Operations Committee: Chairman Jim Floor

Members: Barbara Walters, Jerry Meadows, Brian Hays, Dave Taylor, Angelo Nardone, Glen Baker, Brad Doyle, and Tom Payne

Hearing Committee: Jody Victor, Chairman; Don Wilson, Co-Chairman

Original Members of the Technology Development Group

Dave and Chris Bock, Julie Szuminski, Glenn and Laura Veach

Dave Dougherty, Brian and Denise Udell, Mark and Pat Costello, Gary Brincat, Bob Richardson, Mike Butler, and Brad Doyle

SO HERE YOU are in the Digital Age, but you don't know your mouse from your modem or an Internet from an Intranet—yikes! Luckily, this book has an easy-to-understand guide to some of the more common Digital Age terms.

Bandwidth: a way to describe the amount of information that can move through an electronic network; usually measured in bits-per-second. Companies like AT&T are aggressively trying to increase bandwidth so that more information can flow to your computer faster.

Banner Ad: an advertisement that appears on a Web page, usually across the top of the page like a banner. Banner ads are nearly always hypertext, meaning that you can click on them and they will instantly take you to the site that is being advertised.

Bit: short for binary digit; a bit is a single digit, either a 1 or a 0. All computers are based on a digital format, which means that everything they do breaks down to a language of 1s and 0s.

Bookmark: a way of remembering a location on the Web so you can go back there. Bookmarks are also known as "Favorites" or "Hot Lists," depending on the browser you use.

Byte: a byte is made up of bits, usually a set of eight bits; for example, a byte could look like this—10010101—and might represent something you see on your screen. (**Kilobyte** is a thousand bytes; **Megabyte** is a million bytes. It's ultimately a way of talking about how many 1s and 0s your computer can handle.)

Cyberspace: a term coined by science fiction writer William Gibson, in his award-winning novel *Neuromancer* (1984); Gibson wrote of a worldwide information network called the Matrix, which offered a virtual reality experience called Cyberspace. Today *cyberspace* is used to describe the world of the Internet—when you are online, you are "in cyberspace."

Download: the process of moving information (like software or e-mail) from the Internet to your computer.

Ecommerce: short for electronic commerce; examples include an automatic teller machine and bar code scanning devices in grocery stores; usually used to described Internet-based commerce. Internet-based ecommerce includes business-to-consumer transaction sites (online shopping), business-to-business sites, and paid subscription sites, or "content" sites, that offer information or entertainment.

E-Mail: short for electronic mail; messages you can send back and forth to other people or businesses on the Internet. E-mail operates a lot like normal mail (referred to as "snail mail" in the Digital Age since it's so much slower)—you write a note, address it, then mail it off, where it is opened and read the next time the receiver checks his or her mailbox. E-mail is different from an **Instant Message Service**, which allows you to instantly talk (or "chat") back and forth in writing with other people on the Net. A **Chatroom** is a place on the Internet where you send and receive instant messages from people, usually in groups.

FAQ: short for Frequently Asked Questions; many Internet sites will provide a FAQ that fills you in on what's going on.

Hit: whenever your computer links to and requests to download a certain Web page on the Internet, that is known as a hit.

Homepage: usually refers to the Web page that initially comes up on your screen when you first link to the Internet (which can be changed to whatever you want it to be). *Homepage* is also used to described the main, starting Web page for any site, like the site's front door. For example, http://www.quixtar.com is the homepage for the entire Quixtar site.

HTTP: stands for HyperText Transfer Protocol; http makes it possible to move hypertext information around on the Internet.

Hypertext: text and images that can be used as **Links**, or one-click connections to other Web pages and sites on the Internet. The links, or hypertext, are usually a different color than the regular text around them. The World Wide Web is based on using Hypertext and so it depends on hypertext transfer protocol (http).

Information Superhighway: a term used to describe the World Wide Web, popular in the early 1990s.

Internet: a global interconnected network of tens of thousands of computer networks; it started out as one computer network, the ARPAnet, around 1970.

Intranet: a private computer network (sometimes made up of multiple networks), usually owned by a corporation or a government agency for use by their employees only.

ISP: stands for Internet Service Provider; a service (usually a for-profit company) that allows your computer to connect to the Internet. America Online is a well-known ISP, but there are a number of fast-growing local and regional ISPs as well.

Modem: short for modulator/demodulator: a device that allows your computer to link up with the Internet and talk to other computers through the phone lines. A modem changes (modulates) your computer's digital language into sound (analog) language so that it can travel over the phone lines. On the other end, another modem changes the sound back (demodulates) into digital-speak so that another computer can understand the message.

Mouse: a device that sits next to your computer, which controls the movement of a cursor (usually a little arrow) on your computer screen. Use your fingers to click the mouse and make things work on the screen. See the mouse's long tail going back behind your computer or into your keyboard? A mouse lives on a **mouse pad**.

Net: short for the Internet.

Netizen: a citizen of the Internet; someone who makes use of and participates in the Internet, conducting him- or herself responsibly without intentionally harming others.

Online: a term used to describe the act of being connected to the Internet; as opposed to offline.

PC: short for personal computer.

Portal: one of the main doorways to the Internet. Many big portals (like Yahoo and AOL) had their start as search engines or ISPs but have since become versatile information and commerce sites. Quixtar.com is best understood as a Personal Shopping Portal, a personalized access point to shopping on the Internet.

Pure Play: a term commonly used to describe ecommerce sites on the Internet that do not have a brick-and-mortar counterpart. For example, Amazon.com would be a pure play venture, while barnesandnoble.com would not.

Search Engine: helps you find what you are looking for on the Web. Yahoo, Alta Vista, HotBot, Infoseek, and Excite are all well-known search engines.

Site: a location on the Internet; usually a collection of Web pages that are linked together under the same topic or theme.

Spam: junk e-mail. **Spamming** is the process of mass-mailing junk e-mail to numerous e-mail addresses at the same time (Spam is also the name of a processed meat product manufactured by the Hormel Foods Corporation).

Surfing: as in "surfing the Net": moving around from place to place on the Internet, using hypertext links. "Surfing the Internet" was coined by librarian Jean Armour Polly in 1992.

Tridigital Commerce: a Digital Age business model pioneered by Quixtar.com; it combines an ecommerce Personal Shopping Portal with exclusive member benefits and a unique business opportunity that utilizes affiliate-referral advertising.

Web: short for the World Wide Web.

Web Browser: a computer program that makes it easy to go from site to site on the World Wide Web. The two most popular browsers these days are Microsoft's Internet Explorer and the Netscape Navigator.

Web Page: what you can see on your screen at one time while online; one page on the World Wide Web. One or more Web pages make up a site.

World Wide Web (www): a program designed by physicist Tim Berners-Lee in 1990, which allows hypertext information to be posted and transferred over the Internet.

Chapter 1: You Are Here: The Internet and 10,000 Years of Innovation

THERE ARE A number of terrific books that deal with the history of technology and innovation and how these influence social life. For this chapter I principally relied on: Fernand Braudel's *The Structures of Everyday Life*, Arnold Pacey's *Technology in World Civilization*, T. K. Derry's and Trevor I. Williams's *A Short History of Technology*, Jared Diamond's Pulitzer Prize–winning *Guns, Germs, and Steel: The Fate of Human Societies*, and James Burke's engaging *The Day the Universe Changed*. Jack Larkin's *The Reshaping of Everyday Life, 1790–1840*, provided wonderful insights into the Industrial Revolution. And Olivier Zunz's *Making America Corporate, 1870–1920*, is one of the best studies of the Corporate Revolution I have yet encountered.

Chapter 2: A Short History of Computers in Ten Easy Steps

HISTORY OF COMPUTER resources abound, both on and off the Web. I'd start with *Computer: A History of the Information Machine*, by Martin Campbell-Kelly and William Aspray. One of the richest histories ever written of the computer revolution, it was invaluable to my research. It is also one of the best sources to help you understand how the

Corporate Revolution relied on the use of new office equipment. *Computer* is a must read for anyone in the Digital Age. It also has wonderful photos of all the old computers, including Charles Babbage's difference engine.

A great place to start online is www.pbs.org/nerds, a companion site to the PBS special "Triumph of the Nerds: The Rise of Accidental Empires," which focuses on the development of electronic computers and the personal computer revolution. It has terrific pictures of early personal computers as well.

For a guide to other published histories, as well as a thoroughly detailed computer history timeline, check out www.davros.org/misc/chronology.html. (I apologize in advance if any of these links are no longer posted.) Other notable online sources worth a visit include the University of Minnesota's Charles Babbage Institute (www.cbi.umn.edu); the Computer History Museum at www.computerhistory.org; and www.maxmon.com/history.htm.

Data General maintains an online tour of computers since 1960, at www.dg.com/about/html/generations.html. Lucent Technology presents the must-see, easy-to-follow story of the transistor at www.lucent.com/ideas/heritage/transistor. And the Intel Corporation tells the history of the microprocessor and the birth of the personal computer at www.intel.com/intel/museum/25anniv—definitely a trip worth taking.

One of the most superb online resources that tracks computer statistics and Internet growth is research scientist Brad Myers's award-winning Computer Almanac: (sorry for the long address) www.cs.cmu.edu/afs/cs.cmu.edu/user/bam/www/numbers.html—you'll be glad you stopped by. Computers

Today: *PC Magazine OnLine,* May 1998; *Newsweek,* April 5 and May 31, 1999; Intel Corporation.

Chapter 3: The Internet and Electronic Commerce

FAR AND AWAY the best history of the Internet available today is Stephen Segaller's *Nerds: A Brief History of the Internet,* the full-length book version of an enjoyable PBS special by the same name. I'd also recommend the companion Web site at www.pbs.org/opb/nerds2.0.1.

Other than that, the best sources for the history of the Internet are, appropriately enough, online. I'd recommend starting at www.imcpl.lib.in.us/intronet.htm, which has a lot of rich links; then try http://gale.mines.edu/pangis/hist.html; www.geocities.com/~anderberg/ant/history; and if you want to see a picture of the first computer on the ARPAnet, go to http://millennium.cs.ucla.edu/LK/Inet/birth.html.

Read the true story of how librarian Jean Armour Polly coined the metaphor "Surfing the Internet," and read her original 1992 article at her home page, www.netmom.com— it also includes 100 kid-friendly Web sites. Tracking the Net: some of the best online resources that follow the growth of the Internet include:

- The Internet index, available at www.openmarket.com/intindex/index.cfm
- www.mit.edu/people/mkgray/net/
- www.statmarket.com/
- www.euromktg.com/globstats/

Ecommerce statistics by Industry:

Automobiles
Business 2.0, September 1999; J. D. Power & Associates, as reported in *USA Today,* July 21, 1999; Forrester Research, 1999.

Books
Wired magazine, June 1999: "Barnes and Noble's Epiphany"; *Fortune* magazine, June 1999: "Title Fight", and *Red Herring* magazine, September 1999.

Drugstores
Fortune magazine, July 19, 1999: "Drug Test". Jupiter Communications forecast, reported at CyberAtlas, July 20, 1999.

Real Estate
NPD Online Research, as reported in *USA Today,* August 19, 1999; *The Industry Standard,* June 11, 1999: "Open House: Realtors Learn to Love the Net"; *Business 2.0,* September 1999.

Banking and Financial Services
Dataquest as reported at InternetNews.com, August 10, 1999; GAO findings as reported by Reuters at CNET NEWS.com on August 54, 1999; *Wired* magazine, September 1999, IDC analyst Paul Johnson.

Stocks and Investing
MSNBC, July 28, 1999: "Life Online: Giving Up the Day to Trade Online"; Reuters, August 17, 1999; Harris Interactive News Release, June 1999; *Fortune* magazine, August 2, 1999:

"E*Trade's Plan for World Domination"; Business Week, June 28, 1999: "Where No Frills Net Trades Are Sacred".

Chapter 4: Quixtar's Historical Roots

CHARLES PAUL CONN has written two excellent books on the partnership of Rich DeVos and Jay Van Andel, *The Possible Dream* and *Promises to Keep,* both of which provided a great deal of the background information for this chapter.

I especially want to thank Jody Victor, who graciously made himself available by phone and e-mail throughout my research to answer many questions about Quixtar's historical roots. This book could not have been written without his unselfish assistance.

James W. Robinson has written a recent study of the DeVos/Van Andel success story entitled *Empire of Freedom,* which I also found quite useful.

John Love's *McDonald's: Behind the Arches,* is not only a masterful account of the history of the global fast-food powerhouse but also one of the best histories of twentieth-century American commerce—an exceptional book in every way. Much thanks to Tom Murphy for sending this treasure my way.

Chapter 5: A Star Is Born

DOCUMENTING THE MAKING of Quixtar.com would have been impossible if not for the generous assistance of numerous Quixtar leaders, all of whom candidly shared their memories of the process. John Parker, director of business relations at Quixtar, was an essential source as well.

Chapter 6: Synergy and Advantages

SOURCES CITED IN Twenty Advantages: 1. *American Demographics,* June 1999: "Who's in the Home Office?"; CyberDialogue research; 2. Gates, chapter 5: "The Middleman Must Add Value"; 3. Williams interview: July 30, 1999; 4. Rush interview: July 28, 1999; 7. *Business 2.0* magazine, August 1999: "Quixtar!" by Todd Lappin; 8. DeRose interview: July 1, 1999; Jupiter Communications research as reported at Nua Internet Surveys (www.nua.net) on November 13, 1998; Shelley Taylor & Associates reported at Nua, February 26, 1999; no-sales figure as reported at Nua on June 8, 1999; 9. Schwartz, page 27; 11. *Business 2.0* magazine, September 1999, by Ilene Fischer and Deirdre Frontczak; 12. Schwartz, page 199; 13. *Business 2.0,* August 1999: "Offline, on Message;" Opinion Research as reported at Nua on May 27, 1999: "Word-of-Mouth Drives Ecommerce"; 14. *New York Times* magazine, July 11, 1999: "Instant Company" by Po Bronson; 16. Stephens interview: July 14, 1999; 18. Gates: pages 79, 89; Schwartz: page 46; 19. Harris interview: July 1999.

Chapter 7: The Quixtar Model

HAGEL AND ARMSTRONG, page 12; Malone and Laubacher, "The Dawn of the E-Lane Economy," *Creating Value in the Network Economy,* ed. Tapscott; *Fortune,* May 24, 1999: "The Ascent of E-Man," by Paul Krugman; Hammer, *Atlantic Monthly* magazine, August 1999; McGovern at thecaringeconomy.com; Paynter, *Working Mother* magazine, June 1999: "Workplace 2020"; there is an excellent online history of bicycles at www.channel1.com/users/jcoate/thesis/

chap_2.html and check out the awesome pictures of the earliest bicycles in the Bicycle Museum at www.bicyclemuseum.com; Berners-Lee, as quoted in Segaller, 1998: page 291.

Internet and E-Commerce Sources as Referenced in Chapter 3

ALREADY, JUST OVER 100 million people are online in the United States and Canada. And the number of Internet users worldwide is fast approaching 200 million (Nua Internet Surveys, available at www.nua.net).

There are now well over five million Web sites, up from 26,000 in 1993 (ABC News August 15, 1999).

How many U.S. households go online every hour? 760 (The Internet Index, May 31, 1999)

In the year 2000 an estimated 327 million people around the world will be Internet users (Computer Industry Almanac, July 1999).

Senior citizens are one of the fastest growing segments of the population that are rushing to be part of the Internet (Activmedia, March 26, 1998).

Ninety percent of the 112,000 schools in the United States are online, including more than a third of K–12 classrooms (*Forbes*, July 5, 1999).

Computers are used by 63 percent of adults in the United States, each of whom spends an average of fifteen hours a week using them—six hours of which are online (Harris Poll, 1999).

By the year 2002, 2 million people will be taking college courses online (*Business Week*, August 9, 1999).

Nearly half of those online say that high-speed Internet access is the number one thing they will look for in their next home (*Industry Standard,* August 16, 1999).

By the year 2005, analysts believe there will be over 77 million children and teenagers online all around the world (Nua Ltd., July 1999).

By the year 2005, 60 percent of all the people online will speak a language other than English (Computer Economics Research, July 1999).

In 1999, the top 100 ecommerce Web sites reported annual growth rates of 1,000 percent—a figure that is expected to increase (Activmedia Research, May 1999).

The Internet economy generated more than $301 billion in total revenue in 1998 and was responsible for creating 1.2 million jobs (Commerce Department report released August 17, 1999, follow-up to a study conducted by the Center for Research on Electronic Commerce at the University of Texas).

By the year 2003, business-to-business ecommerce is projected to rocket from $43 billion in 1998 to $1 trillion (Forrester Research, as reported in *Business 2.0,* September 1999).

Business-to-consumer ecommerce is predicted to jump from $7.8 billion in 1998 to $108 billion by 2003 (Forrester Research. as reported in *Business 2.0,* September 1999).

Nearly one-third of all Internet users shop online (CDB Research & Consulting Inc., August 11, 1999).

Analysts estimate that the money spent to advertise on the Internet will soar from $3.2 billion in 1999 to $11.5 billion by 2003. That figure could reach $22 billion by 2004—making advertising on the Internet even more popular than on the radio (Jupiter Communications, August 1999, and Forrester Research, August 1999).

In 1998 an estimated six million households shopped regularly online. By the year 2010 that figure is projected to be 20 million households (Peppers and Rogers Group/Institute for the Future, July 1, 1999).

Total online revenues could exceed $1.3 trillion by 2003 (Activmedia Research, June 7, 1999, as reported at Internetnews.com).

Approximately 427,000 small businesses went online between 1998 and 1999. Seventy-one percent said the Internet was "essential to their success" (Cyber Dialogue Market Research, May 21, 1999, as reported at Internetnews.com).

From 1995 to 1998 the IT industry, even though it accounted for only 8 percent of America's gross domestic product, accounted for 35 percent of the country's economic growth (*The Economist,* July 24, 1999).

Companies worldwide are expected to save over $600 billion a year by 2002, as they reduce or eliminate traditional business costs by going online (Giga Information Group, August 5, 1999).

By the year 2002 teens will account for 1.2 billion in sales over the Internet, and kids aged 5–12 will account for $100 million (Jupiter Communications, August 22, 1999).

By the year 2003 an estimated 95 percent of college students will be online and spending $4 billion a year (*Industry Standard,* August 6, 1999).

Braudel, Fernand. *The Structures of Everyday Life,* trans. from the French by Sian Reynolds. Berkeley: University of California Press, 1992.

Burke, James. *The Day the Universe Changed.* Boston: Little, Brown, and Company, 1985.

Campbell-Kelly, Martin, and William Aspray. *Computer: A History of the Information Machine.* New York: Basic Books, 1996.

Conn, Charles Paul. *The Possible Dream.* New York: Berkley Books, 1977.

Conn, Charles Paul. *Promises to Keep.* New York: Berkley Books, 1985.

Diamond, Jared. *Guns, Germs, and Steel: The Fates of Human Societies.* New York: W. W. Norton & Company, 1997.

Derry, T. K., and Trevor I. Williams. *A Short History of Technology: From the Earliest Times to A.D. 1900.* New York: Dover Publications, 1960.

Gates, Bill. *Business @ the Speed of Thought: Using a Digital Nervous System.* New York: Warner Books, 1999.

Hagel, John, III, and Arthur G. Armstrong. *Net.gain: Expanding Markets Through Virtual Communities.* Boston: Harvard Business School Press, 1997.

Kaku, Michio. *Visions: How Science Will Revolutionize the 21st Century.* New York: Anchor Books, 1997.

Larkin, Jack. *The Reshaping of Everyday Life, 1790-1840.* New York: Harper & Row, 1988.

Leer, Anne. *Masters of the Wired World: Cyberspace Speaks Out.* London: Pitman, 1999.

Love, John F. *McDonald's: Behind the Arches.* New York: Bantam Books, 1986.

Pacey, Arnold. *Technology in World Civilization.* Cambridge: The MIT Press, 1996.

Robinson, James W. *Empire of Freedom.* Rocklin, CA: Prima, 1997.

Schwartz, Evan I. *Webonomics: Nine Essential Principles for Growing Your Business on the World Wide Web.* New York: Broadway Books, 1997.

Segaller, Stephen. *Nerds: A Brief History of the Internet.* New York: TV Books, 1998.

Seybold, Patricia B. *Customers.com: How to Create a Profitable Business Strategy for the Internet and Beyond.* New York: Times Books, 1998.

Tapscott, ed. *Creating Value in the Network Economy.* Boston: Harvard Business Review Books, 1999.

Zunz, Olivier. *Making America Corporate, 1870–1920.* Chicago: University of Chicago Press, 1990.